Continue your adventure in history with three FREE historical novels from James Rada, Jr.

Visit *jamesrada.com / newsletter-email*
and enter your email
to receive your FREE novels.

To Mom,
My No. 1 Fan

SECRETS OF WASHINGTON COUNTY

Little-Known Stories & Hidden History
Where Western Maryland Starts

Other books by James Rada, Jr.

Non-Fiction
- Battlefield Angels: The Daughters of Charity Work as Civil War Nurses
- Beyond the Battlefield: Stories from Gettysburg's Rich History
- Clay Soldiers: One Marine's Story of War, Art, & Atomic Energy
- Echoes of War Drums: The Civil War in Mountain Maryland
- The Last to Fall: The 1922 March, Battles & Deaths of U.S. Marines at Gettysburg
- Looking Back: True Stories of Mountain Maryland
- Looking Back II: More True Stories of Mountain Maryland
- No North, No South: The Grand Reunion at the 50th Anniversary of the Battle of Gettysburg
- Saving Shallmar: Christmas Spirit in a Coal Town

Black Fire Trilogy
- Smoldering Betrayal
- Strike the Fuse

Secrets Series
- Secrets of Catoctin Mountain: Little-Known Stories & Hidden History Along Catoctin Mountain
- Secrets of Garrett County: Little-Known Stories & Hidden History of Maryland's Westernmost County
- Secrets of the C&O Canal: Little-Known Stories & Hidden History Along the Potomac River
- Secrets of the Gettysburg Battlefield: Little-Known Stories & Hidden History from the Gettysburg Battlefield

Canawlers Series
- Between Rail and River
- Canawlers
- Lock Ready

Fiction
- October Mourning
- The Rain Man

SECRETS OF WASHINGTON COUNTY

Little-Known Stories & Hidden History
Where Western Maryland Starts

by
James Rada, Jr.

LEGACY
PUBLISHING
A division of AIM Publishing Group

SECRETS OF WASHINGTON COUNTY: LITTLE-KNOWN STORIES AND HIDDEN HISTORY WHERE WESTERN MARYLAND STARTS

Published by Legacy Publishing, a division of AIM Publishing Group.
Gettysburg, Pennsylvania.
Copyright © 2021 by James Rada, Jr.
All rights reserved.
Printed in the United States of America.
First printing: February 2021.

ISBN 978-1-7352890-1-4

This is a collection primarily of articles that have previously appeared in *The Catoctin Banner, Maryland Life,* and *Hagerstown Magazine.* In some cases where additional information is available the stories have been updated.

Cover design by Grace Eyler.

315 Oak Lane • Gettysburg, Pennsylvania 17325

CONTENTS

Washington County, Maryland 1
County Places 3
   All the Washington Counties 5
   Boonsboro at the Crossroads of History 9
   Funkstown Was a Dream Not Quite Achieved 14
   The Towns That Would Be D.C. 19
   Rethinking the C&O Canal 24
The County at War 31
   The Daughters of Charity at Antietam 33
   The Second Battle of Antietam 45
   How Antietam Was Remembered Fifty Years Later 54
   An Ocean-Going Hagerstown 58
   Washington County in the War of 1812 61
   Fort Frederick Served in Three Wars 67
Interesting People 71
   Getting to the Top the Hard Way 73
   The Last Canallers 79
   An Unlikely Freedom Fighter 86
   The Return of a Ritchie Boy 90
   Keedysville's Choice Twenty-Five Times 94
Crime & Punishment 97
   Hagerstown's Draft Riots 99
   The Unsolved Murder that Haunted Hagerstown 103
   The Last Person to Suffer a Hanging Offense 108

Making Mountain Dew, White Lightning, ... 113
   Hooch, Moonshine
Monsters & Mayhem 119
   The Hunt for the Snallygaster 121
   Western Maryland's Earthquake Capital 127
   The Flood to End All Floods 130
   Washington County's Deadliest Killer 138
Odds & Ends 145
   Amphibian Love Made Hagerstown Famous 147
   Hagerstown's Blues, Terriers, Champs, & Hubs 151
   The Lone Mission of Coxey's Navy 159
   The Woodpecker vs. Fort Ritchie 166
   The World's Largest Organ Manufacturer 169
   When Did People Start Watching TV in the County? 175
   Washington County Enters the Auto Age 179
   Building a Better Road 184
Acknowledgments 187
About the Author 189

Washington County, Maryland

Many consider Washington County as the beginning of Western Maryland. When Prince George's County formed in 1696, it included the area that would eventually become Washington County.

The first settlers arrived in the county in the 1730s and stayed because of the abundant natural resources and fertile farmland. Fort Frederick, built in 1756, helped protect these settlers during the French and Indian War.

Frederick County and points west in Maryland broke off of Prince George's County in 1748, and Washington County broke away from Frederick County on September 6, 1776, making Washington County only two months younger than the United States of America.

Residents chose the county's name to honor Gen. George Washington, who was leading the Continental Army to defend the United States's newly declared independence at the time. It is the first county in the country named after George Washington, and it was at a time before Washington was President of the United States or had led the Continental Army to victory against the British. In naming the county after him, residents declared themselves firmly in support of the new nation and independence.

The county is also home to the first completed Washington Monument. The monument near Boonsboro was completed in 1827, two years before the Washington Monument in Baltimore and fifty-eight years before the completion of the famous Washington Monument in Washington, D.C.

Throughout its history, Washington County has played a role in many famous events from the Whiskey Rebellion to John Brown's Raid to the World Wars. The National Road, C&O Railroad, and Western Maryland Railroad connected the county to the rest of the country and aided its development.

Today, the county has one city, Hagerstown, and eight towns: Boonsboro, Clear Spring, Funkstown, Hancock, Keedysville, Sharpsburg, Smithsburg, and Williamsport.

It also has three national parks, seven state parks, and lots of stories. Some are well known, such as the Battle of Antietam. Others are less well known. *Secrets of Washington County* contains some of these stories.

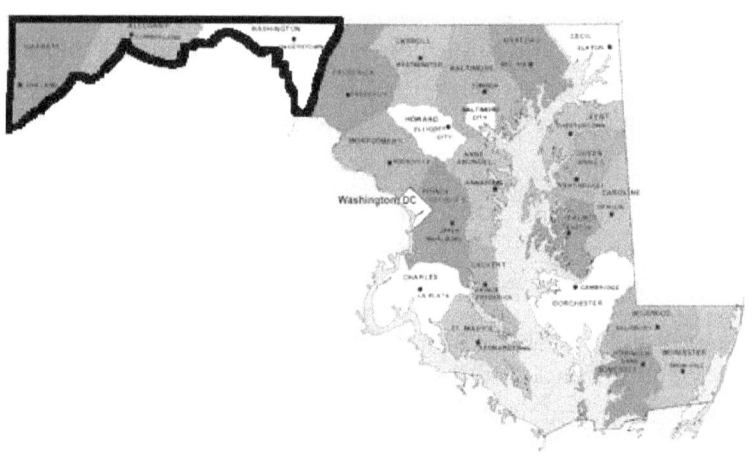

This Maryland State Highway Administration map shows Western Maryland outlined in black. This is also the original Washington County before Allegany County formed in 1789 and Garrett County formed from Allegany County in 1872.

COUNTY PLACES

All the Washington Counties

Washington County may be a great place to live, but it is not unique. The United States has thirty-one Washington Counties, all named after George Washington. This doesn't even count the district named after him, Washington, D.C. However, Washington County, Maryland, is the first place to come up with the idea.

Inspired by the United States breaking away from England and declaring itself independent, Washington County broke off of Frederick County on September 6, 1776. This makes it the first county named in honor of George Washington, who was only known as the commander of the Continental Army at the time.

The second Washington County in Virginia wouldn't come into being until three months later. Although New York and Rhode Island have Washington Counties created before 1776, these counties were originally named something different. Charlotte County in New York was created in 1772 and became Washington County, New York, in 1784. Kings County in Rhode Island was created in 1729 (three years before George Washington was born) and became Washington County, Rhode Island, in 1781.

Here is a list of all the states that have a Washington County and the year their Washington Counties were created:

        1. Alabama - 1801
        2. Arkansas - 1828

3. Colorado - 1887
4. Florida - 1825
5. Georgia - 1784
6. Idaho - 1879
7. Illinois - 1818
8. Indiana - 1814
9. Iowa -1838
10. Kansas - 1857
11. Kentucky - 1792
12. Louisiana - 1819
13. Maine - 1789
14. Maryland - 1776
15. Minnesota - 1849
16. Mississippi - 1827
17. Missouri - 1813
18. Nebraska - 1854
19. New York - 1772 (renamed Washington County in 1784)
20. North Carolina - 1799
21. Ohio - 1788
22. Oklahoma - 1907
23. Oregon - 1843
24. Pennsylvania - 1781
25. Rhode Island - 1729 (renamed Washington County in 1781)
26. Tennessee - 1777
27. Texas - 1837
28. Utah - 1856
29. Vermont - 1811
30. Virginia - 1776 (in December, three months after Maryland)
31. Wisconsin - 1836

Three Washington Counties no longer exist.

Washington County, District of Columbia, formed from parts of Montgomery and Prince George's counties in Maryland. It contained the City of Washington, the City of Georgetown, and unincorporated areas. When the District of Columbia Organic Act of 1871 passed, the county and city governments merged into one district government.

Washington County, South Dakota, formed in 1883. In 1943, it became parts of three other counties because of financial problems in the state.

Washington District, North Carolina, formed in November 1776 (two months after Washington County, Maryland) and existed for a year. The citizens wanted to be part of Virginia, but the state turned down their application. North Carolina then annexed it. After the Revolutionary War, it was part of an unrecognized state, a territory, and finally Tennessee.

Seal of Washington County, Maryland.

Among all the Washington Counties, Maryland's may be the only one (other than the District of Columbia) to have a monument to George Washington within its borders.

The Washington Monument, though started later than Baltimore's Washington Monument, is the first completed monument to the first President of the United States. The citizens of Boonsboro built the monument in 1827, and it is part of Washington Monument State Park. It stands forty feet tall near the summit of South Mountain's Monument Knob.

The first completed Washington Monument near Boonsboro. Photo courtesy of Wikimedia Commons.

Boonsboro at the Crossroads of History

The year 1776 was the year of independence. The American colonies were engaged in a war of independence. Prospects did not look good, but a group of visionary men met in Philadelphia to proclaim the colonies united and free from Great Britain's control. Washington County also broke away from Frederick County and proclaim its own independence and name itself after the general leading the colonies' fight for independence. And a young man named William Boone moved from Berks County to Washington County to settle his own homestead.

From these actions grew a mighty nation, a thriving Western Maryland county, and the small town of Boonsboro.

William Boone and Daniel Boone shared a grandfather (George Boone). Also, William's mother, Sara, was John Lincoln's sister. John Lincoln was Abraham Lincoln's great-grandfather. William married Susanna Parks in 1778. The following year, the Boones moved to a log cabin on a 100-acre farm. The farm surrounds what is now Potomac Street in Boonsboro.

Founding a town

By 1791, Boone began buying additional land, starting with 140 acres along the wagon road from Frederick to Hagerstown.

"We're in a good location," said George Messner, president of the Boonsboro Historical Society. "The topography and geography are ideal. We're located midway between Frederick and Williamsport, which made it a stopover point for travelers."

The Commercial Hotel on South Main Street in Boonsboro around 1915. Photo courtesy of C. D. Young and the Boonsborough Museum of History.

Boone's brother George also moved to Washington County, and the two Boone men began planning a town on their property. The center of town was marked where the wagon road intersected another wagon road to Sharpsburg was marked. The brothers laid out forty-four half-acre lots along that road, which became Main Street.

The first lot (no. 5) was sold for five pounds to Frederick

Netal on November 11, 1792, thus marking the beginning of Boones Berry. However, all the lots were recorded in the county courthouse as Boonesberry Town or Town of Boons Berry.

The town then went through an identity crisis as its name changed to Margaretsville (in honor of George Boone's wife), Margaret Boones Ville, Boonesborough, and Boonsboro.

"Boonsboro had its early heyday because it was the source of several springs," Messner said.

William Boone died in 1798, knowing the young town of Boonsboro would continue his legacy. He and his wife are buried behind the Trinity Reformed United Church of Christ on Potomac Street.

The town grew slowly at first. Although a hotel was built and a post office established in 1801 (Hotel proprietor Peter Conn was also named the first postmaster), Boonsboro only had twenty-four houses by 1803.

U.S. birthplace of macadam

The town's growth spurt began with the construction of the National Road from Cumberland to Baltimore. Main Street became part of the new road.

Construction of the National Road, considered the first federal public works project, began in Cumberland in 1811 and reached Vandalia, Ohio, in 1839. Around the same time, companies were chartered to build a turnpike from Baltimore to Cumberland. The completed turnpike brought wagons filled with settlers and other travelers through Boonsboro.

As part of the construction, macadam was used to finish the last unfinished section of the turnpike from Boonsboro to Hagerstown. John McAdam, a Scottish engineer, developed the material in 1820. It was a state-of-the-art paving technology that quickly spread throughout the United States, but it was first used in the country on a 10-mile stretch of turnpike near Boonsboro.

With the turnpike completed, the town quickly grew to 707 people by 1830. With a sizeable population, Boonsboro incorporated and held its first election in 1831. Its population now includes around 3,700 residents.

Washington Monument

"The biggest highlight of the town was when the citizen of Boonsboro on July 4, 1827, marched up to Blue Rock and began erecting the first monument in honor of George Washington," Messner said.

Most of the town's 500 citizens at the time assembled at the center of town at 7 a.m. "Behind the Stars and Stripes and stepping spiritedly to the music of a fife and drum corps, they marched two miles up the mountain to the monument site," according to the monument's website.

After a full day's work, the monument stood fifteen feet high on a 54-foot circular base. The day ended with a reading of the Declaration of Independence and a three-round salute fired by three Revolutionary War veterans.

The stone monument was eventually completed in September and stood thirty feet high. Baltimore's Washington Monument wouldn't be completed for another two years, and the Washington Monument in D.C. was completed in 1885.

The Battle of Antietam

During the Civil War, the larger buildings in Boonsboro were used as temporary hospitals when the deadliest day in U.S. history took place nearby during the Battle of Antietam.

"A lot of troops went through here on their way to Antietam," said Boonsboro Mayor Howard Long.

The town also cared for wounded soldiers from the Battle

of South Mountain that took place before Antietam. Boonsboro found itself between these two battles.

Saving history

The Boonsboro Historical Society has gathered many oral and written histories of long-time or former residents of Boonsboro. Luana Goodwin, a former resident of the town, spearheaded the effort to save the stories of Boonsboro, its buildings, its residents, and their lives.

"You have to give our people credit," said Long. "They have worked hard to make the town what it is."

The Bowman House built in 1827 is a historic log home on Main Street in Boonsboro. It is currently the home of the Boonsboro Historical Society. Photo courtesy of Wikimedia Commons.

Funkstown Was a Dream Not Quite Achieved

Funkstown is known as a small town of less than 900 residents, and it has never been much larger than that. Town founder Henry Funk had bigger dreams for his land, but his timing was always off.

"Henry Funk, founder of Funkstown, missed the chance to found his nation's capital," the *Hagerstown Daily Mail* reported in 1962.

"He also missed the chance to found the county seat of Washington County.

"But he never gave up hope."

Frederick Calvert sold Funk an 88-acre land grant in 1754 for "one cow hide and other considerations," according to the *Hagerstown Morning Herald* in 1974. Funk called the parcel "Black Oak Ridge," and it was where present-day Funkstown is located.

According to Whilbr.org, this was one of a number of parcels of land Funk would own or come to own in the county.

Henry Funk owned the following lands:
- The 54-acre tract "Walnut Bottom" purchased in 1751.
- The 489-acre tract "Resurvey on Pt. of Simmons Racket" purchased in 1754.
- The 1,086-acre tract "Locust Bottom" purchased in 1758.

- The 31-acre "White Oak Bottom" with David Funk purchased in 1767.
- The 330-acre tract "Resurvey on Harrods Profit" purchased in 1784.

The same Henry Funk may not have owned all these properties, though. Henry Funk is also listed as purchasing two additional parcels in the late 1790s after Funk was known to have left the county. This list also does not include Black Oak Ridge.

Henry Founk (one of the variations of Funk) purchased Black Oak Ridge, according to county land patents. Henry Fouck is also listed as owning:

- The 54-acre tract "Shippays Mistake" purchased in 1749.
- The 25-acre tract "Black Oak Bottom" purchased in 1759.

Funk didn't start out wanting to create a town named after him. He built a mill on Black Oak Ridge" in 1762. This is the same year Jonathan Hager established Elizabethtown, naming it after his wife (this would become Hagerstown in 1813).

Funk's brother Jacob, who also owned many parcels in the county, is credited with laying out a town on Black Oak Ridge in 1767 and naming it Jerusalem. The town grew slowly, though, with the first house not being built on the tract until 1769.

At some point, Funk took a more active interest in seeing Jerusalem grow.

One story was that it rivaled Hagerstown for the county seat "but the personal influence of General Daniel Heister and other leading citizens interested in Hager's Town was supposed to have swung the decision in favor of that community," according to the *Morning Herald* in 1953.

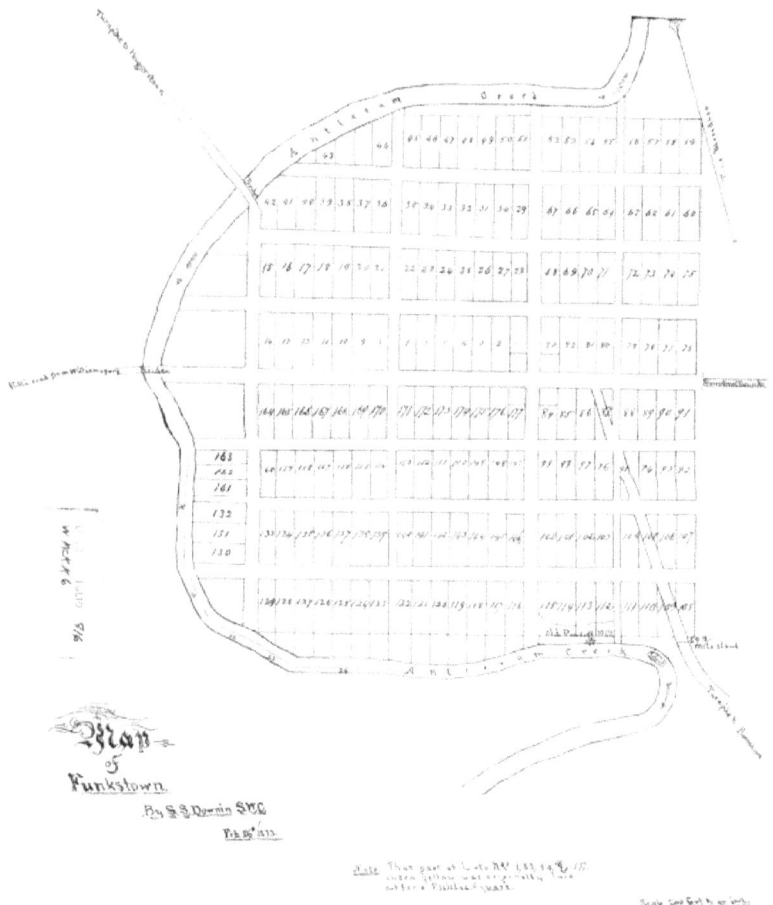

An 1873 map of Funkstown. Courtesy of Funkstown.com.

This story is suspect since the town that received the second-most votes for the county seat was Sharpsburg.

"Oddly enough, though, had Funk utilized his Black Oak Ridge as a town site earlier, the positions of Hagerstown and Funkstown could have been juxtaposed today," the *Morning Herald* suggested. This is because Funk purchased Black

Oak Ridge eight years before Elizabethtown was founded.

Some stories suggest that the town's failure at becoming the county seat led to Funk focusing his attention on other property he owned along the lower Potomac River.

In the 1780s, he tried to establish a community that he called at different times Funkstown and Hamburg. It wasn't as attractive to settlers as Daniel Carroll's nearby Carrollsburg, though. Funk finally gave up his dream in disgust and moved back to Washington County.

"If he had stayed on, would our nation's capitol (sic) be called, 'Funkstown, D. C.'?" the *Daily Mail* asked.

This is because his land soon became incorporated into the District of Columbia.

Having lost out once because he didn't act soon enough and once because he acted too soon, Funk stopped trying to create towns. He did find some success, though. Although Jersusalem would not be renamed Funkstown until 1810 when the town was incorporated, people were already starting to call it that.

In 1791, a local newspaper reported, "families to the number of about fifty person in and near Funkstown took their departure for Kentucky; also, that good old man, Mr. Funk, late a representative of this county, went with his baggage."

That was the last anyone in the county ever heard of Henry Funk.

"He was determined to establish a town that would become city of importance – and he took the determination, unrewarded, with him to his grave," the *Morning Herald* notes.

However, he and his brother did leave behind a town that continues, which is something not many people can say.

An old postcard showing the bridge over Antietam Creek that connects Funkstown and Hagerstown.

The Towns That Would Be D.C.

The first U.S. Congress, which met in 1789, had a lot of decisions to make. It set the benchmarks that other Congresses would be measured against. Each representative and senator also wanted to see federal money spent in their districts.

One, if not the largest, prize was where to locate the nation's capital. As the seat of the federal government, it would be where a lot of money was spent. Not only that, but businesses would benefit from all of the people who would work and live in the capital city.

The names of well-known cities were suggested. Princeton, New Jersey. York, Pennsylvania (which had served at the capital city for a short time during the Revolutionary War). Williamsburg, Virginia.

The locations were narrowed down when Secretary of the Treasury Alexander Hamilton and Secretary of State Thomas Jefferson were said to have reached an agreement over dinner. Hamilton needed the support of Jefferson and James Madison in order for his plan to have the federal government assume all state debt accumulated during the Revolutionary War. States that had paid off a large portion of their debt did not support this plan because they would be subsidizing the poorer states. Jefferson and Madison wanted to see the nation's capital located in the South, which the northern states did not support.

Hamilton agreed to help Jefferson and Madison get the votes necessary to locate the capital city in the South, while Madison agreed to help pass Hamilton's federal assumption of debt plan.

Congress passed the Residence Act in July 1790 which declared the capital city would be somewhere along eighty miles of the Potomac River from the Anacostia River to Williamsport, Md., near Hagerstown. Suddenly, towns in Montgomery, Frederick, and Washington counties, which hadn't been considered earlier, were now in the running as the location for the seat of the United States Government.

The act granted President George Washington the power to choose the final location. The U.S. Constitution also set the size of the site to be no greater than ten square miles.

This no doubt pleased Washington. Not only was his home, Mount Vernon, located on the Potomac, but the river had fascinated him from a young age. He believed it was the key to growing the nation westward.

Although Washington had his own ideas about where the capital city might be located, he set out on October 15, 1790, to listen to representatives from other towns make the case for their location as the best place for the seat of the federal government.

"By moving farther up the Potomac, that thoroughfare to the western region, the situation will be more healthy, it will add to the cultivation of an extensive, fertile, and populous country, and it will be more accommodated to our fellow-citizens west of the mountains and more so to almost one half of Pennsylvania, than if the seat of government was at Philadelphia," W. B. Bryan wrote in *History of the National Capital*.

Bryan makes the case that Washington County would have been a good choice because of its central location, it closeness to stores, iron furnaces, and factories.

It is believed Washington reached Shepherdstown, Va., on Oct. 19. The residents of Shepherdstown and Sharpsburg had raised pledges of land and money totaling $25,000 to locate the federal city around Sharpsburg and Antietam Creek.

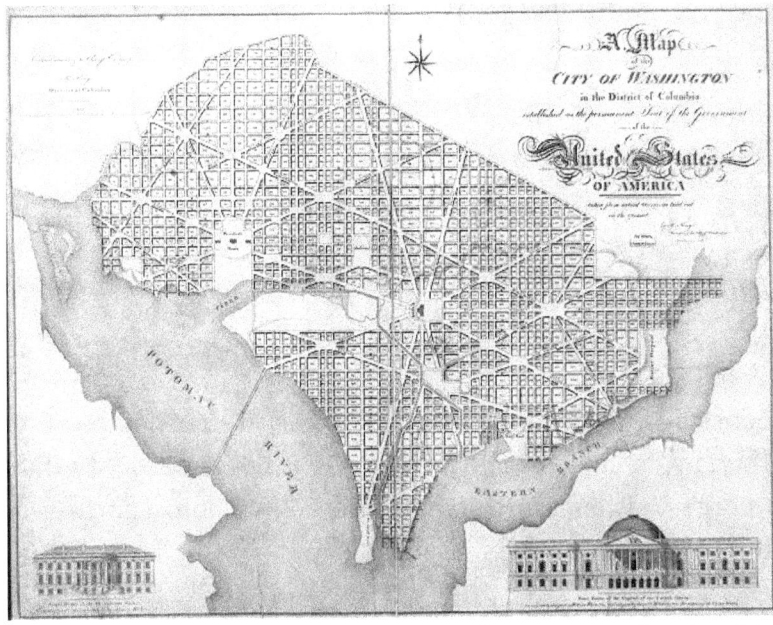

A map of the City of Washington in the District of Columbia that would become the permanent seat of government. Photo courtesy of the Library of Congress.

From his visit there, Washington traveled to Hagerstown the following day. According to the National Archives, "The president was escorted into town by the local militia, presented with a welcome address, and honored with a public dinner, followed by the usual thirteen toasts. One, in particular, expressed the tenuous nature of the Residence Act: 'May the residence law be perpetuated, and Potomac view the Federal City.' GW is said to have lodged at Beltzhoover's Tavern, more formally known as the Globe Inn, and proceeded up the Potomac the following morning."

He then traveled to Williamsport to view the land and hear what the town fathers had to say.

Construction of the U.S. Capitol dome in Washington, D.C. This might have happened in Washington County had George Washington thought differently. Photo courtesy of the Library of Congress.

By Oct. 24, Washington had returned to Mount Vernon. Soon after, a handbill signed "An Inhabitant" circulated through the county. Titled "The Residence Act and the recent visit of the President," it sought to "encourage the Citizens of Washington County to hope that the Seat of the Federal Government will be located therein; And while the Citizens of other Counties on the Patowmack, have the same expectations, and will probably contribute considerably towards the construction of the necessary buildings, an inhabitant of Washington County invites his Country-men to make similar exertions. Partial or limited conditions annexed to a Subscription on this occasion, would divide the interest of the

County into so many parts, favouring particular places, as to render the amount of any one of the Subscriptions of small consideration; He therefore recommends that the only condition to be annexed be 'that the permanent Seat of the Federal Government be located by the President in Washington County…'"

By the end of the year, President Washington had made his decision, and although no one knew what it was, many suspected the federal district would be around Georgetown.

On January 24, 1791, President Washington issued a proclamation fixing the boundaries of the new federal district. The capital would be a square measuring 10 miles on each side, although oriented on a map it would appear in the shape of a diamond. It was also the furthest south location in the range along the Potomac Congress set. Many in Congress had wanted a location further upriver, but what they didn't realize was that the Washington and his family owned thousands of acres in the district. Although no one accused Washington of making his decision for his own self-interest, he certainly benefited from it.

Congress met for the first time in the new capital on November 17, 1800, but the transfer of the federal government from Philadelphia to Washington City wasn't completed until June 1801.

Rethinking the C&O Canal

The old saying goes, "You can't fit a square peg in a round hole." Yet for more than ninety years, historians have said that somehow ninety-two-foot-long canal boats on the Chesapeake and Ohio Canal fit into locks that could hold boats no larger than ninety feet and probably less.

It's just one of the many questions that modern researchers are finding need to be answered about the C&O Canal. Some have easy answers that go against the accepted history of the canal. Others, like the question of canal-boat length, are still being researched.

Both have historians and National Park Service staff rethinking how the C&O Canal operated.

The C&O Canal ended business operations in 1924. Since then, books have been written about the canal, historians have researched the lives of canallers and lock tenders, and the National Park Service has documented the life of the canal. You would think that in that time, all that could be known about the canal had been discovered. It turns out that that's not the case.

"New information available and things are happening remarkably quickly," said Karen Gray, a C&O Canal National Historical Park historian.

The work being done is the transcription of canal records, historic newspaper articles, and other canal documents, primarily by William Bauman, a member of the C&O Canal Association. Gray vets a lot of the information. Some pieces are posted on the C&O Canal National Park Service site, but she puts most of the information on the C&O Canal Association website in the "Canal History" section. The section includes oral histories, newspaper reports from long-forgotten newspapers along the canal, books, reports, payroll records, canal boat registration documents, and family histories.

"William Bauman has done a lot of terrific work collecting and transcribing records and articles to give everyone a flavor of how the canal operated," said Bill Holdsworth, who is both the president and webmaster for the C&O Canal Association.

The C&O Canal Association is a volunteer organization that promotes and advocates for the canal.

"There's so much available, but it needs to data mined," Gray said.

A careful reading of this new information has turned some long-held beliefs about the canal on their heads.

For instance, it has been written that canal boats in the 1800s were privately owned and often operated by a family. While they often were privately owned, "It was written into the boat mortgages that the boat needed to operate twenty-four hours a day," Gray said. "A family is not going to be able to do that."

Holdsworth said this is the most-surprising thing that he has learned from the new information. "Canal work was not this leisurely, bucolic life of strolling along the towpath," he said. "Those people were working hard and moving fast along the towpath."

Records show canallers make the trip along the canal in roughly four days.

Gray explained that the idea of family run boats comes

primarily from a 1923 U.S. Department of Labor study that was conducted at a time when sixty percent of the canal boats were run by a family.

The lock at the Great Falls Tavern Visitor Center on the C&O Canal.

In addition to boats not being family run, evidence suggests that a single captain might have been in charge of up to four boats. What is not certain at this time is whether those boats moved together or one towed another boat or some other variation, but the records don't support the one boat– one captain idea.

"It's really clear that we need to rethink our original beliefs of how the canal operated," Gray said.

In her own study, she divides the canal into the three periods. The first period is the time up until the canal opened to Cumberland. During this point, the canal was being built, but it had partial operation to different types of boats. From 1850 to the turn of the century, the canal operated independently for the most part and also had its golden age. From the turn of the century until the canal closed, it operated primarily under the Canal Towage Company at a reduced capacity.

The research has even turned up a couple mysteries that have yet to be solved.

Before the canal was fully completed to Cumberland in 1850, flatbed riverboats used to travel the Potomac River and enter the partially open canal at the dam near Williamsport. From there, they could continue their journey to Georgetown.

The question is how did they continue their journey? Riverboats were carried by the current with the crew using poles to guide the boat. Poles could not be used on the canal, though, or the clay berm would have been damaged. So how were the boats moved through the canal?

"Most likely, someone rented mules at Williamsport, but we don't know for sure," Gray said.

Perhaps the biggest mystery is how canal boats that were supposed to be ninety-two-feet long fit into some locks that could hold boats no longer eighty-five to ninety feet. The ninety-two-foot boat length comes from a single boat that was used to make drawings from. At the time the drawings were made, the boat had been out of the water for years so it is probable that frame may have loosened somewhat, adding length and width to the dimensions. This is only a guess at this time, though.

A National Park Service employee acts as a mule walker along the C&O Canal at the Great Falls Tavern Visitors Center.

"All of this information is a great resource that we've been able to make available to the world so that future researchers and future students can did down and do deep analysis," Holdsworth said.

He said that since much of the current beliefs about the canal come from oral histories of canallers and information from the canal's last days, this new information is changing people's impressions of the canal.

Catherine Bragaw, chief of interpretation for the C&O Canal, said that rangers are always looking for stories that people can relate to and that as more research becomes available, it may change the stories.

"It's not unusual for history to change," Bragaw said. "Some history stays consistent. Some is dynamic as more is uncovered."

Canalling did not generally become a family business until the 20 century. Photo courtesy of the Library of Congress.

She said that interpretation is an art because different people can focus on different aspects of the subject. That, in turn, affects, the stories and information they incorporate into their presentations.

"It's fascinating to unlock the mysteries," Bragaw said.

That's just what this new research continues to do. It is unlocking the mysteries of the early days of the canal and discovering new ones that need to be solved.

THE COUNTY AT WAR

The Daughters of Charity at Antietam

As the Confederate Army crossed the Potomac River and marched north in September 1862, it soon became clear they were heading towards Frederick, Maryland, in the center of the state. They took control of the city, expecting an enthusiastic welcome as a liberating army.

That wasn't what happened, though. "We were rather disappointed at our reception, which was decidedly cool. This wasn't what we expected…There was positively no enthusiasm, no cheers, no waving handkerchiefs and flags—instead a death-like silence—some houses were closed tight, as if some public calamity had taken place," wrote Confederate infantryman Alexander Hunter.

In the meantime, Major General George B. McClellan had gathered the Army of the Potomac and headed after the Confederate Army. Lee took his army west over South Mountain.

General McClellan caught up with General Lee's army on South Mountain and the two armies began fighting. The Confederate Army tried to block the Union at the mountain passes without success. McClellan's men pushed through the passes and over the mountain.

The Confederate Army retreated, and Lee considered

heading south. But with General Stonewall Jackson's capture of Harpers Ferry on Sept. 15, General Lee made a stand at Sharpsburg.

Maryland authorities had already requested help from the Daughters of Charity to help with the wounded on the day of the battle. "The people of the area were asked to help the Confederate soldiers, and the Sisters and people of Emmitsburg collected clothing, provisions, remedies, and money," according to *Annals of the Civil War*. This is a collection of first-hand accounts of the sisters' Civil War experiences.

The Daughters of Charity had nearly thirty years of health care experience. During the Civil War, they cared for soldiers in both the North and the South.

A view of St. Joseph's Academy during the Civil War. The Union Army would camp in the fields around college in the days before the Battle of Gettysburg. Courtesy of the Library of Congress.

On Sept. 17, a foggy morning, cannons and rifle fire erupted between the towns of Boonsboro and Sharpsburg. So began a twelve-hour battle that would became deadliest single day for America. Nearly 100,000 soldiers fought, and by day's end, nearly 23,000 were casualties.

The following day the work began saving the wounded and burying the dead.

Father James Francis Burlando, director of the Daughters of Charity during the Civil War. Photo courtesy of the Daughters of Charity.

The Daughters of Charity

Elizabeth Ann Seton founded the Sisters of Charity of St. Joseph's in 1809 in Emmitsburg. It was the first order of religious women native to the U.S. Their primary mission at the time was education, but they soon expanded into healthcare. This began in 1823 when the sisters took over the management of nursing services of the Baltimore Infirmary and five years later, they opened to the first Catholic hospital west of the Mississippi River.

This was unique at the time. There were no professional nurses. Many believed nursing was not a suitable profession for women. Relatively healthy hospital patients or the poor acted as nurses in public hospitals. No formal training program existed and most nurses either learned their skills by providing care to family members or assisting a doctor to whom they were related.

They gained experience working with victims of violence, accidents and cholera in Baltimore, Philadelphia and Boston during outbreaks in 1832-1833 and 1850. They also became well respected for their abilities.

The Daughters of Charity had been providing nursing care to Confederate even before the outbreak of the war. Sister Regina Smith ran the Charity Hospital in Louisiana for the state and Daughters of Charity. A group of four men approached her in late March 1861 and asked the Daughters of Charity to provide care for ill Confederate soldiers. This was about two months after Louisiana had seceded from the Union and a month after the Provisional Confederate Congress met and formed the military and two weeks before the bombardment of Fort Sumter.

When war finally broke out, Daughters of Charity were in both the North and South in the Union states of New York, Massachusetts, Pennsylvania, Wisconsin, Michigan, Illinois, Maryland and California. In the Confederate States, they served in Louisiana, Mississippi, Alabama, Missouri and Virginia.

Dorothea Dix

Neither the Union nor the Confederacy was ready to care for those who survived the battles wounded and maimed at the start of the Civil War. They received volunteer help from various aid societies that formed after the start of the war and more-formal help with the appointment of Dorothea Dix as the superintendent of U.S. Army nurses.

However, Dix's authoritarian and biased management style won her no friends. No woman under thirty years old need apply to serve in the government hospitals. All nurses were required to be plain-looking women. Their dresses had to be brown or black with no bows, no curls in their hair, no jewelry, and no hoop skirts. But for these requirements, there may have been more women accepted as nurses.

Though these requirements would seem to fit many of the Catholic sisters and nuns serving in the war, Dix also had a "no Catholics need apply" proviso. So the Daughters of Charity operated independently and doctors found them a pleasant alternative to Dix and her nurses. Plus, the Daughters were the most experienced nurses in the country. They had been nursing and administering hospitals for decades and they had dealt with large-scale public health crises like yellow fever and cholera.

The Daughters at Antietam

Father Edward Smith, C.M., pastor in Emmitsburg, drove two sisters to Boonsboro in a wagon. They arrived at twilight after the battle's end and found four hospitals for Union wounded and three for Confederate wounded. "But as the fighting had been over twelve or fifteen miles space, the towns of Boonsboro and Sharpsburg were hospitals," wrote Sister Matilda Coskery.

When the Daughters of Charity arrived, two Union officers recognized the sisters by their cornettes and one said, "Ah, there come the Sisters of Charity; now the poor men will be equally cared for."

Calling the sisters Sisters of Charity or Sisters of Mercy was a common mistake people made. The terms were used interchangeably for Catholic sisters and nuns at the time.

Although the Daughters of Charity started out as Sisters of Charity in 1809, they affiliated themselves with the Daughters of Charity in France in 1850. The most visible change in this affiliation was the clothing worn by the sisters. They adopted the blue-grey dress, white collar and white cornette of the Daughters of Charity. It's this wide cornette that became their signature and one reason they were called the angels of the battlefield.

The sisters headed immediately to the battlefield to search for wounded among the many dead bodies. On their way there they found all the houses and barns being used as hospitals with the wooden fencing, where there was still any left, draped with bloody clothing. The wounded lay on the ground with only a bit of straw for a mattress. If they were lucky, a blanket might have been stretched out on sticks driven into the ground to provide shade. Otherwise, they had had no protection from the sun during the day as they suffered from their wounds.

The sisters set about to improve the conditions of the wounded by distributing the goods they had brought with them. Sister Matilda wrote of the soldiers, "Unable to move or change their position, every filth surrounded them; add to this, vermin, maggots and stench. Bullets could be gathered from between them, that lay scattered around."

This would have been particularly troubling to her because she had written repeatedly about the need for cleanliness not only of the patients but also of the utensils and medical instruments that touched the patient and the sick room that surrounded him.

The wounded were already being transferred to hospitals, not only in Boonsboro, but in the larger cities of Frederick and Hagerstown as well.

Mother Ann Simeon led the American Daughters of Charity during the Civil War. Photo courtesy of the Daughters of Charity.

All around them, the Daughters of Charity saw devastation. The crops had been trampled, the fences had been used for fuel, livestock had disappeared, and even the dogs were killed or had fled from the appalling scene. Sister Matilda wrote of the scene, "…that on no battlefield during the war were any of those carrier (sic) birds seen, not even a crow; though piles of dead horses lay here and there, some half-burned from efforts made to consume them by lighting fence rails on them—but these seems rather to add to the foulness of the atmosphere than to help purify it."

When the supplies the sisters had brought with them were used up, they told one surgeon, "We are sorry. We have nothing to offer you but poor sympathy."

"Oh," replied the surgeon, "the sympathy of a Sister of Charity is a great boon to our soldiers at any time."

The sisters found themselves "in constant danger from bomb shells which had not exploded and which only required a slight jar to burst. The ground was covered with these and it was hard to distinguish them when the carriage wheels were rolling over straw and dry leaves," according to George Barton in *Angels of the Battlefield*.

The battle's 23,000 casualties nearly overwhelmed the sisters' ability to help them. Someone always seemed to need their attention. No matter how fast they helped one soldier, two more were waiting.

With so much death around them, the sisters had little patience for anyone trying to add more. At one point, a Union steward and Confederate surgeon got into an argument on the battlefield that escalated to the point where one challenged the other to a fight to the death on the battlefield that was already saturated with blood. As both men left to duel, yelling at each other, one sister followed. She dressed them down and took their pistols from them. Ashamed, the men returned to their posts and resumed their work, according to Barton.

The sisters approached one mortally wounded soldier in a wagon shed. An officer told them the man had been a hero as a flag bearer during the fighting.

"I fear the man is dying rapidly; come to him," the officer said. "He has been so valiant that I wish to let his wife know that the Sisters of Charity were with him in his last moments."

And so the sisters remained with him. Father Smith arrived to give the man last rites. With the sisters near, the soldier faced his death with a courage matched by what he had shown in battle.

The Union medical director sought to thank the sisters for coming to the aid of the soldiers and asked them to dine with him at dinner. The sisters tried to decline, but the officer wouldn't take "no" for an answer. So they joined him at his dinner table and ate "spoiled pork and war biscuit, the dinner, with tea in bowls large enough for bleeding purposes, and much we feared they were used for that purpose!" Sister Matilda wrote. Instead, the sisters withdrew some provisions they had brought and ate an unspoiled meal.

Following the meal, "Night drove us to our lodgings in the town before we were ready for it but returning to the same field the next morning, those we had assisted the day previous, were consigned to the earth; and they that could not consent yesterday to receive baptism, now eagerly received it," Sister Matilda wrote.

One man "consigned to the earth" was the flag bearer who the Daughters of Charity had seen die the day before. Besides the sisters and Father Smith, about ten others attended the service.

According to Barton, a group of horsemen approached the sisters during the funeral and removed their hats.

One man said, "I am General McClellan and I am happy and proud to see the Sisters of Charity with these poor men. How many are here?"

"Two," one sister answered. "We came here to bring relief to the suffering and we return in a day or so."

"Oh, why can we not have more here?" General McClellan asked. "I would like to see fifty sisters ministering to the poor sufferers. Who shall I address for this purpose?"

Father Smith supplied the general with a name and address where he could send the request. Then McClellan asked after the welfare of the flag bearer.

When he was told that the flag bearer was about to be buried, McClellan joined in the funeral procession.

Though the Daughters of Charity intended to stay only a few days, they wound up staying three weeks, washing, dressing wounds, baptizing, feeding, and praying for thousands of wounded men.

Nuns of the Battlefield

Of the 700 Catholic sisters and nuns from twenty-two orders known to have provided some sort of service in the Civil War, the largest number came from the Daughters of Charity. They served in just about every state involved in the war and on many of the battlefields.

Many of the soldiers who received care from the Daughters of Charity during the Civil War never forgot their battlefield angels or the care the sisters gave them.

After the war, Sister Mary Conlon's remains were exhumed from Point Lookout, Md., where she had died of typhoid fever and taken to Washington City for reburial in Calvary Cemetery. The soldiers who assisted with the exhumation and reburial showed the remains a great reverence while they handled them.

On December 13, 1862, Union soldiers had attacked the Confederate stronghold called Marye's Heights. Thomas Trahey of the Sixteenth Michigan Volunteers was wounded in the fighting and taken to an emergency hospital. There Sister Mary Louise La Croix cared for him until he was well enough to return home.

After the war, Trahey wrote to the Central House asking after Sister Louise. He was told that she had died two years after the war had ended and was buried in St. Louis. Trahey located her grave and began making an annual pilgrimage there.

On October 15, 1874, Catholic Sisters Josephine Meagher and Rachel Conway, were chosen to unveil a monument at former President Abraham Lincoln's tomb in Oak Ridge Cemetery in Springfield, Illinois. The memorial recognized the service of the Catholic sisters in the war.

On September 20, 1924, a marble and brass memorial called "The Nuns of the Battlefield" was dedicated in Washington D.C. to all the religious orders that provided nurses during the Civil War. The monument is at the intersection of Rhode Island Avenue NW and M Street NW, opposite of St. Matthew's Cathedral. The Ladies' Auxiliary of the Ancient Order of the Hibernians paid for the monument.

Archbishop William Cardinal O'Connell told the audience, "Should the time ever come that this nation faced the horrors of war… Then, too, will come out of their cloistered homes another band of ministering angels, the spiritual heirs of holy nuns, whose sacred memory we here venerate, and they, like those here honored, will bring to the fallen aid and consolation, courage and resignation."

The Nuns of the Battlefield Memorial in Washington D.C. Photo courtesy of the Library of Congress.

The Second Battle of Antietam

Early in the morning of August 25, 1924, more than 3,000 Marines under the command of Brig. Gen. Dion Williams marched onto waiting barges at the Marine Camp Quantico in Virginia. At 4 a.m., the Navy tug boats towed the barges up the Potomac River toward Washington, D.C. Meanwhile, tanks and artillery pieces towed by trucks rolled out along the Richmond Road headed for the same place.

Their ultimate destination was Sharpsburg. Sixty-two years after the historic battle, the bloodiest day of the Civil War was soon to be re-fought.

Saving the Corps

Despite having proven themselves to be fierce and effective warriors during World War I, politicians and some military leaders began talking about disbanding the U.S. Marine Corps after the war ended. Maj. Gen. John A. Lejeune, commandant of the U.S. Marine Corps, understood that his Marines needed to fight for survival in the political arena just as hard as they fought on the battlefield. He devised a campaign to raise public awareness about the Marines.

One way he did this was instead of going to obscure places to conduct war games and train, he chose iconic places and put the Marines out in front of the public. At the time, the national military parks and battlefields, such as Antietam, were still under control of the U.S. War Department, which meant the Marines could use the parks as a training ground.

Lejeune did just that with a series of annual training exercises that started in 1921 with a re-enactment of the Battle of the Wilderness. The following year, the Marines marched to Gettysburg, and in 1923, they refought the Battle of New Market.

Marines take a break in the 1924 re-enactment of the Battle of Antietam. Photo courtesy of the Library of Congress.

The march

The week-long march to Sharpsburg retraced most of the route that the Marines had taken two years earlier when they went to Gettysburg. They marched from Washington, D.C. through Bethesda, Rockville, Ridgeville, and Frederick before reaching Sharpsburg. Unlike previous years, the Marines got to ride in trucks for much of this march.

One time they were required to march was crossing South Mountain. They walked across the mountain so the trucks would have an easier time climbing the grades. Even then, some trucks had to drive to Sharpsburg by way of Hagerstown because they were too heavy to cross the bridge at Keedysville.

Navy reconnaissance balloons were used to observe the progress of the 1924 Battle of Antietam. Photo courtesy of the Library of Congress.

Even in trucks, the Marines were an impressive sight, and they garnered a lot of public support and positive publicity during the march. Along the way, the Marines drew crowds that watched them march past. They also invited visitors into their camps to hear the band play or simply to talk with the Marines. Occasionally, they played baseball against local teams, and they always sought out any living Civil War veterans to invite them to come to Gettysburg and watch the re-enactments as a guest of the Marines.

Marines wore their regular uniforms during their 1924 re-enactment of the Battle of Antietam. Photo courtesy of the Library of Congress.

At Sharpsburg

The Marines reached Sharpsburg on September 1, 1924. The North American Expeditionary Force consisted of the Fifth Marine Regiment (artillery), Tenth Marines (artillery), and engineers, signalers, medical corps, a chemical unit, and an aviation unit.

They set up their camp on the farm of E. E. Piper near Sharpsburg. The aviation group of thirteen planes created a landing field next to the Hagerstown Pike, one mile west of Boonsboro.

"Like ghosts from the past the Marines will move over the field in their formations and maneuvers and will make preparations for a battle on Sept. 12 such as was engaged in by Union and Confederate troops in the Civil War," the *Frederick Post* reported.

Until the re-enactment, the Marines spent their days learning about the battle of Antietam, as well as modern training. Cold weather and rain hampered them at times. On Sept. 3, lightning struck the camp switchboard, knocking the phone from the hand of GySgt. Smith.

When the Marines were paid on Sept. 3, half of them went into Hagerstown to watch the Marine baseball team play the Hagerstown Hubs, Hagerstown's class D professional baseball team. The Marines lost that game 8-1, but would go on to win games over the weekend against the Shepherdstown and Sharpsburg Athletic Clubs.

During the night, county residents would often see searchlights panning through the night sky and hear anti-aircraft guns firing as the Marines conducted night drills.

Motorists and tourists during the public events the Marines hosted overwhelmed Sharpsburg and Boonsboro.

An estimated 50,000 people came out to visit the camp on Sept. 7 to watch as the aviation group "did every stunt known to flyers," according to the *Frederick Post*. They also dropped flowers on the graves in the National Cemetery at Sharpsburg.

During each evening leading up to the re-enactment, the Marines demonstrated their capabilities for the public.

The re-enactment

Six days later, the crowd returned in even greater numbers to watch the battle re-enactment. The *Baltimore Sun* reported, "It was the largest crowd assembled here since that September day in 1862 when General Lee matched his forces against McClellan's fighting Yankees. They began streaming in this morning before the marines were away and they continued to arrive until after the battle was over."

Another difference between the 1924 re-enactment from the previous ones was that these Marines wore modern uniforms and equipment rather than trying to portray Civil War soldiers.

Marines charge in mock attack during the 1924 re-enactment of the Battle of Antietam. Photo courtesy of the Library of Congress.

The Sun described the battle this way: "The ground was the same but that was all. Airplanes circled overhead and swooped down low to bomb the 'enemy' lines. Artillery firing blank shrapnel laid down a barrage for an advancing infantry. The infantry deployed and crept forward, while machine guns rattled on either flank. And finally tanks scurried here and there through the enemy lines, spitting fire and leveling positions."

Members of the G. A. R. were given the best seats so that the Civil War veterans could watch the re-enactment, but only one of them had actually fought at Antietam. George W. Conner, 81, of Raspeburg (part of Baltimore City), had fought for the Union in Battery B, First Maryland Regiment of Light Artillery, Second Division.

The Marine encampment during the 1924 Battle of Antietam re-enactment. Scanned from a newspaper story.

Shortly before the battle began, Marines escorted an old man wearing a grey coat to the guest stands. He sat behind Conner, and it was soon discovered that he was eighty-four-year-old Francis Jones, of Charlestown, W. Va. He had served with Gen. J. E. B. Stuart's cavalry division on the Confederate side during the battle and was the only

Confederate veteran in attendance.

When the two men realized they had fought as enemies sixty-two years earlier, "they clasped hands, pulled their chairs closer together, put their arms about each other's shoulders and started a verbal battle of Antietam," *The Sun* reported.

Marines take care of their "casualties" during their 1924 Battle of Antietam re-enactment. Photo courtesy of the Library of Congress.

As the two men watched the battle, Conner was heard to remark, "Look at those boys. You'd think there was a dozen or two of them. Why, when our outfit marched into this battle it went shoulder to shoulder, like it was on a parade. No creeping and falling down like those boys."

They then began recalling their memories of the original battle and seemed not to notice the battle going on in front of them. "I'll never forget that day if I live to be 184," Jones said. "I've done some work in my time, but that was the hardest day's work I've ever put in."

Each one made the argument that he had been on the winning side, even as they walked off together to eat lunch after the battle ended.

The event was deemed a success, and the Marines broke camp to return home the following day.

Despite the popularity of these events, Maj. Gen. Lejeune ended the program after Antietam because of the high costs involved, according to Kenneth L. Smith-Christmas in his *Leatherneck* article about the event. Brig. Gen. Williams, in conjunction with the U.S. Army, restarted the events as part of the remembrance of the seventy-fifth anniversary of the Civil War.

How Antietam Was Remembered Fifty Years Later

The last major anniversary events the Civil War that saw actual veterans in attendance was the seventy-fifth anniversaries. Antietam's 75th anniversary was in 1937.

For Washington County residents, the event also represented the bicentennial of the settling of the county and the 175th anniversary of the founding of Hagerstown. The latter events had been originally planned for 1935, but they had been postponed because of the country's poor economic condition. The money just wasn't there to prepare for a big event.

However, remembering Antietam was not only a big event, but it was a federal one. President Franklin Roosevelt created the National Antietam Commemoration Commission and appointed Maryland U.S. Senator Millard Tydings to chair it, along with members Maryland U.S. Senator George Radcliffe, Maryland Congressman David Lewis, General Milton Reckord of Maryland, Virginia U.S. Senator Henry Byrd, and Vermont Congressman Charles Plumley. Maryland Governor Harry Nice appointed a state advisory committee. Park Loy was the secretary and treasurer of the commission and the chair of the Washington County Historical Society, which handled much of the organization of the events.

The souvenir guide from the 75th anniversary of the Battle of Antietam. It focused on the peace between the North and the South. Photo courtesy of *Whilbr.org*.

As the anniversary date approached, estimates were a quarter million people, including President Roosevelt, would attend.

Events were planned over two weeks from Sept. 4 to 17. Some days were themed like "National Anthem Day," "Baltimore City Day," and "Defenders' Day." At times, the events seemed more appropriate to a county with livestock shows and a carnival midway.

Maryland Motorist Magazine described the events this

way: "For two weeks it will feature a 'junior world's fair' complete with large-scale historical pageant and, on its final and climatic day, will mark the 75th anniversary of the Battle of Antietam by re-enacting that famous struggle on the battlefield—following an address expected to be delivered by President Roosevelt. ... The visitor will find many attractions for his attention. A gala carnival midway, a stately museum overflowing with objects of rare historical interest, a series of villages depicting life in foreign countries, a glorious field of flowers on the approach to the Horticultural Hall, a long Industrial Court displaying some of the earliest curiosities and some of the latest wonders in manufacturing, a Travel Building devoted to the visual store of ancient and modern transportation, the Paradise Gardens where all the animals and all the plants will flourish, a Commercial Building where hundreds of nation wide wholesalers and retailers will spread their wares before the world, and finally the great dramatic spectacle 'On Wings of Time.'"

Twenty-one governors of the twenty-nine states whose troops fought the Battle of Antietam attended the climatic day featuring the re-enactment, along with President Roosevelt. National Guardsmen of Maryland, Pennsylvania, and Virginia re-enacted the "Bloody Lane" phase of the battle. About 1,500 men took part in the re-enactment with 900 of them in the Union army and 600 in the Confederate army.

President Roosevelt spoke to the gathered crowd across from the Dunkard Church where part of the battle occurred. Sharpsburg citizens presented him with a section of a tree hewn on the battlefield. It contained a bullet fired during the battle.

Roosevelt told the audience, "In the presence of the spirits of those who fell on this field - Union soldiers and Confederate soldiers - we can believe that they rejoice with us in the unity of understanding which is so increasingly ours today. They urge us on in all we do to foster that unity in the spirit of tolerance, of willingness to help our neighbor, and of faith in the destiny of the United States."

President Franklin D. Roosevelt at the 75th Anniversary of the Battle of Antietam. Photo courtesy of Whilbr.org.

About fifty Civil War veterans attended the events; most of them in their nineties. Though there were a few thousand Civil War veterans still alive in 1937, less than 100 actually fought at Antietam.

The bitterness of seventy-five years prior had disappeared and "frequently men who fought for the South were seen arm in arm with soldiers of the North," according to the *Hagerstown Morning Herald*. In one picture, ninety-four-year-old Cpl. Bazel Lemley, of the Confederate Army, shook hands with Gen. Benjamin Franklin Red of the Union Army at Bloody Lane where they had tried to kill each other in 1862.

An Ocean-Going Hagerstown

Agerstown became seaworthy in 1945... the *S.S. Hagerstown Victory*, that is.

Early in World War II, the U.S. War Shipping Administration commissioned the design of a new type of cargo ship. It was an enhanced version of the successful Liberty ships. The new ships, which were designated Victory class, were 455 feet long and sixty-two feet wide with a 15,200 ton displacement. This made them slightly larger than Liberty ships and slightly faster, too. The latter was important because traveling at fifteen to seventeen knots made the ships less likely to come out on the losing end of a U-boat attack. For additional protection, the ships had a 5-inch stern gun to defend against submarines and a 3-inch bow gun and eight 20-mm cannons to fight any attacking aircraft.

However, these weren't fighting ships. They were cargo vessels.

The first of the line, the *S.S. United Victory,* launched on January 12, 1944. Although it took a while to ramp up production (only fifteen ships had launched by May 1944), by the end of the war, 531 Victory ships had been built. After the *S.S. United Victory*, the next 34 ships were named after Allied countries. The following 218 ships were named after American cities. The next 150 were named after educational institutions, and the remainder had miscellaneous names.

The ships fared well in the war. U-boats didn't sink any,

and Japanese kamikaze attacks only sunk three of the ships in 1945.

The S. S. Hagerstown on her launch day at the Bethlehem-Fairfield Shipyard in Baltimore.

Workers laid down the hull for the *S.S. Hagerstown Victory* on December 19, 1944, at the Bethlehem-Fairfield Shipyard in Baltimore. She launched on Feb. 13. The Maryland Legislature appointed a special committee to attend the event. According to the *Hagerstown Morning Herald*, the committee chairman was Robert H. Tenney. The other members were Howard E. Ankeney, Myron L. Bloom, Henry Holzapfel, III, John N. Newcomer, Harry W. Zeigler and J. Claude Johnson. All of them were from Washington County, except for Johnson, who came from St. Mary's County.

The legislature also passed a resolution that read in part, "the people of the City of Hagerstown have made an outstanding and meritorious contribution to the all-out war effort, and in recognition of this achievement, the city has been singly honored by having one of the Victory ship named for it."

The *S.S. Hagerstown Victory* served in the European Theater, traveling to places like Gibraltar, Istanbul, Odessa, Marseilles, and Oran. U.S. Merchant Marines crewed the ship and a contingent of U.S. Navy Armed Guards protected the crew. A complement of USAT (Water Division) also served aboard for troop administration.

In October 1945, the ship was modified to transport up to 1,500 troops rather than cargo. Her cargo holds were converted to bunk beds and hammocks stacked three high. The cargo holds had mess halls and exercise areas added to them.

The *S.S. Hagerstown Victory* then began carrying German and Italian POWs to LeHavre, France, and Antwerp, Belgium, where they were repatriated. On her return trips to America, she carried soldiers who were eager to return home.

Then, on June 15, 1946, after more than twenty trips back and forth across the Atlantic, the *S.S. Hagerstown Victory* became part of the James River Reserve Fleet. Sometimes called a "mothball fleet," a reserve fleet is made up of ships that are fully equipped but are partially or fully decommissioned. The idea being that, if needed, they can quickly be recommissioned and brought back into service.

Washington County in the War of 1812

Some historians call the War of 1812 the second American Revolution. Less than a generation after America won her independence, she once again battled Great Britain. It was a war that neither side wanted because both countries were still recovering from the original American Revolution.

The British fought a defensive war early in the War of 1812 because they were also fighting against Napoleon Bonaparte and the French army and navy in Europe. By 1814, Britain defeated Napoleon and turned their attention to ending the war with the United States. Up to this point, most of the fighting had been around the Canadian and U.S. border to the north. In the Mid-Atlantic, the British had started a blockade in 1813.

"During the years of Madison's administration, from March 1809 to June 1812, the English continued their insults, aggressions, and depredations. Our harbors were insulted and outraged, our commerce swept from the ocean, our seamen impressed into British fleets, scourged and slaughtered, fighting the battles of those who held them in bondage, and studied indignities were offered to our national flag wherever displayed. All efforts for redress from the British government had failed, and at length (acting in accord with a majority of the Senate and House of Representatives of the United States) the President issued his proclamation declaring war against Great Britain on the 18th day of June 1812," J. Thomas Scharf wrote in *History of Western Maryland*.

Preparing for war

Maryland soldiers had distinguished themselves for their bravery and ability during the Revolutionary War. They were so dependable George Washington called the Maryland regiments his "Old Line," which is where Maryland's nickname as "The Old Line State" comes from, according to the Maryland Archives.

However, war is a political question as well as a military one, and Maryland was split over the need to go to war. The Federalists called themselves the "Friends of Peace." Their position was that the U.S. should fight only to defend its borders and not try to take territory from Canada, which had been happening on the northern front of the war. The Democrats were called "War Hawks" and fully supported not only a defensive war but an offensive one.

"As a rule the county [Washington] gave a warm support to the war, although a majority was evidently against its declaration; but when once begun the great body of the people rallied in its favor. Still there were some who steadily opposed it as unwise and unnecessary," Scharf wrote.

In 1812, the Maryland Legislature divided the state into eleven regimental districts, plus one extra squadron. Washington and Frederick counties were in the first district.

By February, officials appointed Capt. Frisby Tilghman the lieutenant colonel in command of the county's regiment, Capt. Otho H. Williams was appointed the regiment's major. Moses Tabbs was elected captain, Jacob Barr first lieutenant, David Clagett second lieutenant, and David Newcomer cornet.

Lt. John Miller, of the United States army, opened a recruiting station at Hagerstown in February, as well. He ran an advertisement for recruits, saying: "Every able-bodied man from the age of eighteen to thirty-five years who shall be recruited for the army of the United States for the term of five years will be paid a bounty of sixteen dollars; and whenever he shall have served the term for which he enlisted, and obtained an honorable discharge, he will be allowed, in addition to the aforesaid bounty, three months' pay and one hundred and sixty acres of land; and in case he should be killed in action or die in the service, his heirs and representatives will be entitled to the said three months' pay and one hundred and sixty acres of land."

During their enlistment, the soldiers earned $5 a month.

Answering the call

Washington County supplied 600 men to the war effort as part of the state's need of 6,000 fighting men. This was when the county's population was not even 19,000 people.

"Every one of them volunteered, making a draft unnecessary," the *Hagerstown Herald-Mail* reported.

Some companies even formed before the War of 1812 in the expectation a war was coming. Capt. John Ragan, Jr. formed the Hagerstown Volunteer Rifle Company in 1807. The following year, captains Henry Lewis, Joseph Chaplain, John Harry, and Daniel Hughes, Jr. all formed their own companies.

Seeing action

The *Herald-Mail* noted that county men saw action on all the war fronts "as far north as Lake Erie and as far south as New Orleans."

Capt. Thomas Quantrill, Maj. Otho Williams, Capt. John

Miller of Sharpsburg, Capt. Wherritt of Funkstown, and Capt. Stevens of Hancock led to their men to help with the defense of Annapolis and Baltimore.

"Most of them were sent home in time to help with the harvest of 1813, then were ordered back to defend Baltimore in 1814," the *Herald-Mail* reported.

Many of them participated in the Battle of North Point on September 12, 1814. Although the Americans retreated, they inflicted heavy casualties on the British and left them demoralized and confused. It also led to a delay in the British attack on Baltimore, which gave the Americans more time to prepare. Quantrill's Hagerstown Volunteers were commended for bravery at the battle.

The Battle of North Point as painted by Thomas Ruckle. Washington County soldiers distinguished themselves during the battle. Photo courtesy of Wikimedia Commons.

Capt. Ragan's company didn't fare as well. They took part in the Battle of Bladensburg. The British routed the Americans during the battle, and it led to the capture and burning of Washington, D.C. However, Scharf notes, "although his command early in the engagement broke and fled in the utmost disorder, he particularly distinguished himself in his brave efforts to rally his raw and panic-stricken troops, but in the fruitless attempt was thrown from his horse, severely injured, and finally taken prisoner by the enemy."

The *Herald-Mail* also noted that Capt. Elliot "shared" in Commodore Oliver Hazard Perry's victory on Lake Erie when an entire British naval squadron surrendered for the first time in history.

Lt. Col. Charles Boerstler of Funkstown wasn't as lucky. He was forced to surrender to avoid the slaughter of the 500 men under his command during the Battle of Beaver Dams.

"There was much discussion in the press as to whether he had been duped by the British into surrendering to a smaller force, or had acted wisely to prevent further loss of men. Boerstler was exonerated by a Court of Inquiry," according to Whilbr.org.

The Star-Spangled Banner

Lawyer Francis Scott Key wrote a poem after watching the British bombard Fort McHenry in Baltimore in 1814. It was eventually set to the tune of a popular British song and titled "The Star-Spangled Banner." It became our national anthem in 1913.

However, the original poem, "The Defence of M'Henry," was originally published in Hagerstown in the *National Songster of 1814*, according to the *Hagerstown Town and County Almanack*, which also owned the publication.

The almanac's website notes, "is that though it appeared in many songsters, the VERY FIRST appearance of the poem as a song under the title, 'Defence of Fort M'Henry', was in 'The National Songster', Hagerstown, Maryland in 1814 with the direction that it be sung to the tune of To Anacreon of Heaven. This publication was the product of John Gruber, founder of The Hagerstown Town and Country Almanack! This has been corroborated by many bibliographies of American Songsters from 1734 to 1820."

John Gruber owned both the *National Songster* and the *Hagerstown Town and County Almanack*, which is the second oldest almanac in the country, and the almanac still published and sold by descendants of its founder.

Fort Frederick Served in Three Wars

Fort Frederick sits between the Potomac River and Interstate 70 in Big Pool. Many people know it played a role in defending Western Maryland against Indians during the French and Indian War. What they don't realize is the fort served in three different American wars spanning 109 years.

When Indians defeated British General Edward Braddock and his troops in western Pennsylvania on July 9, 1755, settlers on the Maryland frontier worried.

"The Indians incited by the French became more and more bold in their raids and attacks upon the settlers, and fires, massacres, scalping and the carrying away of prisoners were of constant occurrence," W. McCulloh Brown wrote in *Maryland Historical Magazine* in 1922.

Maryland Governor Horatio Sharpe and the Maryland Legislature responded to the worries. The Legislature authorized £6000 for a frontier fort, and Sharpe began work on a major fort the following year amid the French and Indian War. He named the fort after Frederick Calvert, who was the Sixth Lord Baltimore. It was large enough to resist an attack and offer nearby colonists refuge if an attack happened.

Besides planning the fort, Sharpe also directed its construction, visiting the site three times in the summer of 1756.

He didn't design it to resist an artillery attack because he assumed correctly the French wouldn't be able to transport artillery to the frontier. Construction took nearly two years. "Mounting expenses finally compelled the assembly to cut off funds in 1758, although the fort does seem to have been substantially complete by that time," according to the Fort Frederick State Park website.

The quadrangle-shaped fort is 355 feet from bastion point to bastion point with eighteen-foot high and three-foot thick stone walls. Inside, there were three barracks buildings.

French and Indian War

Col. John Dagsworthy was the first commanding officer of Fort Frederick. He initially had 150 men, but by November 1758, he had 200 men and six-pound cannons mounted on the fort walls.

"This fort when completed was probably one of the most formidable and strongest along the English frontier, and to this fact owed its immunity from attack," McCulloh wrote. "It was considered as the most westerly point in Maryland that could be successfully defended."

The fort served as a base for supplies. Colonists visited the fort for aid and support. Friendly Indians and officers met at the fort to negotiate and form alliances.

Troops from Delaware, North Carolina, Pennsylvania, and Virginia were all stationed at the fort for a time.

"Although no military action occurred at Fort Frederick during the war, it did serve as an important staging area and supply base for English operations further west. After the fall of Duquesne, the Maryland Forces were disbanded and Fort Frederick was closed," according to the park website.

The park was reactivated in 1763 to protect residents from Ottawa Chief Pontiac's Indian rebellion against the

English. The fort sheltered 700 settlers for a time, although the violence never got near the fort.

Revolutionary War

Although the fort was far from the fighting during the Revolutionary War, it was used as a prisoner of war camp from 1777 to 1783. The fort was refurbished and placed under the command of Col. Moses Rawling. About 1,000 British and German soldiers were kept there after the battles of Saratoga in 1777 and Yorktown in 1781.

"As the years went on the prisoners were allowed much liberty and were even let out to work upon neighboring farms, and discipline became lax," McCulloh wrote. "In 1780 a plot formed by Loyalists or Tories to liberate the prisoners was by accident discovered in time to prevent it."

After that, officials confined all prisoners to the fort.

When the war ended, many of the prisoners remained in Washington County to become citizens.

With no further use seen, the State of Maryland sold the fort to Robert Johnson in 1791 for $1,875.

Civil War

With the outbreak of the Civil War, Fort Frederick was on the border between the North and South. Two Union infantry companies garrisoned in the fort and used as a gun emplacement to protect both the Chesapeake and Ohio Canal and the Baltimore and Ohio Railroad.

"These troops are believed to have knocked a hole in the south curtain wall through which they trained a cannon toward rebel territory across the Potomac. Confederate troops tried to dislodge the Union soldiers but were unsuccessful," according to the park website.

Its use during the Civil War ended in 1862.

A sketch of Fort Frederick from the southwest. Courtesy of the Library of Congress.

Restoring the fort

Fort Frederick remained in private hands until 1922, when the State of Maryland purchased it to use as the first Maryland state park. The Civilian Conservation Corps undertook archeology at the fort and rebuilt the wall and the stone foundations of the interior buildings in the 1930s.

In preparation for the fort's rededication in 1937, the *Connellsville (PA) Courier* noted, "It is the only old fort in America whose walls remain intact to this day. First on the main trail to the great unbroken West, the Fort later became isolated from travelers when the National Pike went through."

Today, the fort offers tours, displays, exhibits, and living history activities.

INTERESTING PEOPLE

Getting to the Top the Hard Way

Men helped George Oakley into a straightjacket and secured the thirty-six-year-old man's arms behind him on the evening of August 25, 1924. The men tied a rope around Oakley's feet, and with a signal, a winch lifted Oakley upside down to the top of the six-and-a-half-story First National Bank Building in Hagerstown. Hanging from a car tire inner tube, Oakley freed himself from the straightjacket, climbed down the side of the building, and then back up to the roof, "Going up the outside wall of the First National Bank Building with the ease of an ordinary mortal climbing the steps inside...," according to the *Hagerstown Morning Herald*.

Before this gravity-defying feat, the daredevil had stood on his head on the front bumper of a Chrysler with four-wheel brakes. The car drove along the street at 10 mph with Oakley appearing as an upside-down figurehead on the car. The car braked, throwing Oakley into the air. He turned a somersault before landing on his feet.

"The reliability of 4-wheel brakes was amply demonstrated when the car came to a halt before touching Oakley, but he also managed to show that he is totally deficient in the quality of fear," the *Morning Herald* reported.

George Oakley was a rare breed of daredevils called "Human Spiders" or "Human Flies" during the first half of the twentieth century. These men traveled the country climbing tall buildings and performing other tricks for amazed audiences. The Human Spider and the sponsoring organization split the money collected from the spectators. During this performance, Oakley earned $22 for the Lions Club Milk Fund.

It was an adventurous life and a dangerous one.

George Oakley's death certificate after his fall in Chambersburg, Pa. Note his occupation is listed as a "House Scaler."

A week after his Hagerstown appearance, Oakley was dead. While climbing Chambersburg Trust building in Chambersburg, Pa., using only a cane and an inner tube, the tube snapped and Oakley fell three stories to the ground. An examination at Chambersburg Hospital showed that Oakley had several broken bones including lower vertebrae, his pelvis, ribs, left arm and his breast bone with many of the bones being broken in multiple places. According to *The Franklin Repository*, his "nervous system suffering much from shock." He suffered for hours before dying from his injuries the next day.

Human Fly Johnny Reynolds juggles while balanced atop a spire. Photo courtesy of the Library of Congress.

This sense of danger made the climbs exciting for spectators. They never knew whether they were watching an unbelievable act of daring and skill or a man committing suicide. Whether such stunts should be allowed was a headache for local governments that issued permits for such climbs. Hagerstown, as well as many other cities, had legislation against such stunts, but often ignored them to help a good cause.

Oakley's death scared Hagerstown officials enough that they started enforcing the city ordinance. When Henry Rowlands wanted to climb either the Dagmar Hotel or First National Bank Building in 1926, the city denied him a permit.

Twenty years later, the Hagerstown government was willing to let things slide once again when Johnny Woods climbed the eight-story Dagmar Hotel for two shows on May 24, 1946. He was successful, and audience collections helped the William D. Byron VFW Post raise money for a new VFW building and the rehabilitation of hospitalized soldiers.

The climb was not much of a challenge to a man who had climbed the forty-two-story L.C. Smith building in Seattle, the twenty-five-story Hotel Pittsburgher in Pittsburgh, the Hearst Tower in Baltimore, and the Tribune Tower in Chicago, among others. However, it was a thrilling spectacle for local residents to witness in person.

Two other Human Flies are known to have performed in Hagerstown. Jack Williams climbed the Dagmar Hotel in 1916. "Only a small cane was used in climbing from the windows of one story to another until he reached the fifth floor where it was necessary to muster a rope in service in order to ascent the cornice which extends a distance of four feet from the main building," the *Morning Herald* reported.

He returned in 1922 to climb the First National Bank building using only his bare hands.

In 1917, Johnny Reynolds climbed the Costello Building on South Potomac Street. "He did all kinds of tricks on the side of the building and when he got to the top, he took four tables and chairs and performed marvelous tricks," the *Morning Herald* reported.

Human Fly Johnny Reynolds performs a stunt on balanced chairs on top of a building. Photo courtesy of the Library of Congress.

Reynolds was twenty-eight years old at the time and had been climbing for half of his life. He had even scaled 543 feet up the side of the Philadelphia City Hall.

Although many of the famous Human Flies were active in the first couple decades of the 20th century, Human Fly John Ciampa climbed buildings in the 1940s and early 1950s, Human Fly George Willig climbed the World Trade Center in 1977, and Human Fly Rick Rojatt was a stunt rider in the 1970s. While daredevil stunts still attract attention, they have become increasingly more dangerous. In 2014, Alan Eustace jumped from a spacecraft in space and fell 25.75 miles safely to earth using only a parachute to slow his descent.

The Last Canallers

On November 13, 1923, the *Hagerstown Daily Mail* let canallers know the Chesapeake and Ohio Canal would close for the winter the following week. While most boatmen had already moored their boats waiting for the water to be drawn from the canal, Pat Boyer, captain of the Canal Towage Company No. 5 boat, pressed on. He dropped off one last load of coal in Georgetown and hurried back to the Cumberland Basin.

Working on the C&O Canal meant your life was connected to a stretch of water that was 60 feet wide and 184.5 miles long running from Cumberland to Georgetown. The path of the canal roughly follows the course of the Potomac River, which supplied the canal with its water supply.

Boyer had had a successful season, as it seemed all the canal boatmen had. The *Daily Mail* reported, "The canal had a busy though shorter season this year than in previous years, it is stated. Not as many boats were operated on the canal this season as in former years, but the demand for coal at Williamsport, Washington and other shipping points kept the fleet of barges going all season."

So when Boyer tied up his boat in Cumberland Basin, he was looking forward to the 1924 boating season, and hopefully, another successful season. He chose his winter port so he would be one of the first boats loaded when the canal opened in 1924.

Next spring came, but the boating season didn't.

The end of an era

What came was rain, and lots of it. On Mar. 28 and 29, 1924, heavy rains pelted the region, melting the snow on the mountains. The snow and rain ran into the creeks and Potomac River.

"By 8:30 a.m. on the 29th, Wills Creek overflowed its banks resulting in tremendous havoc and property loss in the Cumberland vicinity. Telephone, telegraph and electric wires were swept away, and the city left in darkness. Cumberland's central business district was flooded to a height of four feet. Most of the paving washed away with a torrent of water rushing down Mechanic Street at a great velocity," wrote local historian Al Feldstein in the historical commentary of the novel *The Rain Man*.

Contemporary newspaper reports said the waters rose as fast as thirty inches an hour, and the river approached the then-record crest of the 1889 flood.

When the floodwaters receded, officials assessed the damage. "The entire Williamsport division of the Chesapeake and Ohio Canal has been destroyed and may never be rebuilt. For more than 100 years it has been a lane of traffic from Cumberland to Washington, and thousands of tons of coal have been carried down it every year. The flood completely covered it, and when the waters receded Monday it was found that its banks had been obliterated. Officers of the company controlling the canal said they frankly doubted if the damage would ever be repaired," the *Daily Mail* reported.

Talk immediately began about repairing the canal. A Cumberland company won a contract in April to make repairs. Around Williamsport, section foremen also made repairs. The efforts met with little success.

On Aug. 1, the *Morning Herald* announced, "It was decided that it would be useless to reopen it this season, and all employees were discharged. The few boats left are in such condition that they cannot be used again, it is said."

The C&O Canal sits drained and abandoned in Georgetown during the 1930s. Photos courtesy of the Library of Congress.

In the beginning

On July 4, 1828, President John Quincy Adams broke ground for the Chesapeake and Ohio Canal near the Great

Falls in Maryland. The C&O Canal was the fulfillment of George Washington's dream to make water flow uphill. It was the first great national project, and it was a failure.

"The project contemplates a conquest over physical nature, such as has never yet been achieved by man. The wonders of the ancient world, the pyramids of Egypt, the Colossus of Rhodes, the temple at Ephesus, the mausoleum of Artemisia, the wall of China, sink into insignificance before it: —insignificance in the mass and momentum of human labor required for the execution—insignificance in comparison of the purposes to be accomplished by the work when executed," Adams said.

The C&O was a construction and engineering challenging for its time. It involved more than simply digging a trench across level land and making it water tight. Boats traveling from Georgetown to Cumberland had to be lifted over 600 feet on their westward journey.

The laborers were mainly imported Irishman, who jumped at the chance to come to America, though they quickly found the work unsatisfying. The work was hard, and the tools were picks, shovels, horses and black powder.

When completed, the canal had eleven aqueducts, seventy-four lift locks, 160 culverts, and twelve river feeder locks and guard locks.

The problem was that by the time the canal reached Cumberland in 1850, the Baltimore and Ohio Railroad had already been there eight years, though both projects had started on the same day in 1828.

The final project had cost $14 million or $9.5 million more than estimated. According to Elizabeth Kytle in *Home on the Canal*, as a portion of the gross national project, building the C&O Canal was the equivalent to putting a man on the moon.

Throughout its history, the C&O Canal was in competition with the B&O Railroad for business. Photo courtesy of the National Park Service.

A wet money pit

The Johnstown Flood storms in 1889 shut the canal down for more than a year and put it into receivership. The possible sale of the canal was problematic for the B&O Railroad. Not only was the railroad a canal bondholder, the railroad needed the canal to remain open to keep the Western Maryland Railroad from obtaining the canal rights of way that would allow the railroad to press into Western Maryland.

The B&O Railroad arranged to have receivers who supported the B&O Railroad placed in control of the canal, but it still needed to make a profit to avoid being sold. This was not happening, so the railroad started the C&O Transportation Company to create an agreement that would allow the C&O Canal to show a paper profit.

In 1902, the Consolidation Coal Company, which was owned by the B&O, formed the Canal Towage Company. This changed the life on the canal. Captains became employees of the Canal Towage Company and had their boats provided to them by the company. The once-colorful boats with fanciful names now became uniform, with only a number identifying one boat from another.

Then the Western Maryland Railroad found a way into the Maryland mountains, and the B&O's main reason to keep the canal operating vanished. The canal became a financial burden on the railroad, and the 1924 floods gave the railroad a way out.

Some boats hauled sand from Georgetown to the power plant that was being constructed in Williamsport for a few months in 1924, but the damage at Cumberland kept boats away from that end of the canal. Boyer's No. 5 had been the last boat to haul freight on the canal.

In a 1979 interview featured in *Home on the Canal*, Lester Mose, Sr., who had worked on the canal during its last years, said, "The '24 flood took all the boats away. What wasn't taken away in '24 [the] '36 [flood] cleaned them up. There wasn't nothing there. It was dead. Closed up and growed up with trees."

The B&O Railroad sold its rights to the canal to the federal government in August 1938 for $2 million. It was a paper transaction that allowed the railroad to pay off some of its $80 million loan from the federal government's Reconstruction Finance Corp and to borrow another $8.2 million more.

Otho Swain was born on the canal in 1901 and worked on it during its final years. He said in a 1976 interview in *Home on the Canal*, "The canal finally closed down in 1924. There was flood damage then, but the railroad—it was the railroad that really killed the canal."

A canal boat left abandoned after the C&O Canal closed. Photo courtesy of the National Park Service.

An Unlikely Freedom Fighter

"Even on a dying pillow, it will comfort us to think that we have done at least one good act in our lives, that we have been instrumental in establishing religious freedom in Maryland, that we have broken the yoke of superstition and prejudice, and let the oppressed go free, and that we have caused happiness to many an anxious heart."

—Thomas Kennedy

"We hold these truths to be self-evident, that all men are created equal, that they are endowed by their Creator with certain unalienable Rights, that among these are Life, Liberty and the pursuit of Happiness…"

So reads part of the Declaration of Independence, authored in 1776 and the founding document of our country. Yet, that same year, the Maryland legislature set the state constitution to paper and discovered that some men were created a little more equal than others.

The Maryland Constitution noted that "all persons professing the Christian religion are equally entitled to protection in their religious liberty." Later, in Article 35, it read, "No other test or qualification ought to be required on admission to any office of trust or profit than such oath of support and fidelity to the State…and a declaration of belief in Christian religion."

This exclusion of non-Christians from holding public office and from religious protections left Jews as second-class citizens in Maryland.

Luckily, a third thing happened in 1776 that plays a role in this story. The man who would eliminate that religious discrimination was born, and he was not a Jew, but a Presbyterian.

Thomas Kennedy was a Scotsman who came to America in 1795 at the age of nineteen to forge a new life for himself. He married Rosamond Thomas of Frederick in 1802 and built a family home in Williamsport two years later.

Thomas Kennedy

Kennedy developed an interest in religious freedom that spurred him to become active in politics. He was elected to the House of Delegates in 1817 as a representative of Hagerstown.

The following year, Kennedy became a member of the committee considering removing the bias against Jews from the Maryland Constitution. He took up the cause "to consider the justice and expediency of placing the Jewish inhabitants on equal footing with the Christians," he wrote.

Though the anti-Jew provision placed Maryland's constitution in conflict with the U.S. Constitution, it was not a big issue at the time because there were only about 150 Jews living in the Free State. Kennedy, ironically, had never even met one. His outrage came from his belief in religious freedom and the fact that he saw a group being discriminated against because of its beliefs.

In January 1819, "An Act to extend to the sect of people professing the Jewish religion the same rights and privileges that are enjoyed by Christians" got out of committee, but was defeated on the floor by a vote of 24-50. Kennedy would not give up, though. He reintroduced the bill in 1820, and it was again soundly defeated.

Because of his persistence on the issue, Christians branded him an enemy (although he was a Christian himself). The *Hagerstown Torch* called him a "wicked, designing, hypocritical politician; say he's more, had we more names for badness. If we have not already satisfied all candid men that he is all that he had been represented to be, and if possible, even more politically depraved, we do not despair of yet being able to do so."

Kennedy's stance against religious discrimination also cost him his delegate seat. He lost to Benjamin Galloway, a strong opponent of the "Jew Bill," in the 1823 election.

Still, Kennedy was overcome with righteous indignation and would not give up the fight even when out of office. He wrote, "Although exiled at home, I shall continue to battle for the measure, aye, until my last drop of blood."

He ran for the House of Delegates again in 1825 and was elected as an independent. His hard work paid off in another way: Public opinion toward the non-Christian bias in the state constitution turned, and Kennedy's bill passed in 1826. Just a few months later, two Jews were elected to the Baltimore City Council.

Having achieved his goal, Kennedy retired from public office and helped found the *Hagerstown Mail*, a newspaper of which he would become the editor.

His days in office were not through, however. He was called on to serve out the term of a state senator who had died in office, which he did for five years, until 1831. At that time, he decided he preferred being a delegate and was re-elected to that position.

Kennedy died in October 1832, a victim of the cholera epidemic ravaging the area.

In 1918, some of Maryland's Jewish citizens erected a monument to Kennedy in Hagerstown. Its inscription reads simply: "One who loved his fellow man."

The Return of a Ritchie Boy

Cascade may be a small community nestled in the mountains, but what happened there during World War II helped changed the world.

Guy Stern fled Nazi Germany in 1937 as a young man of fifteen. He left behind his parents and two siblings.

"I made efforts to get the papers for my family to emigrate and I almost succeeded, but in the end it did not work," said Stern in an interview with the *Waynesboro Record Herald*. Stern's family eventually perished in the Holocaust.

Meanwhile, Stern attended St. Louis University and was drafted into the U.S. Army in 1942. Only a few months after his basic training in Texas, he received secret orders to transfer to Camp Ritchie in 1943.

Because of his German heritage, the army had selected him to take part in a military intelligence training program. Using the knowledge of the German language and culture that men like Stern had, they were trained in interrogation, psychological warfare, and counter-intelligence. About 9,000 mostly Jewish soldiers went through the training and became known as The Ritchie Boys.

Stern was trained in interrogation techniques, the evaluation of enemy documents, psychological warfare, German propaganda and ancillary skills that every soldier needs. The training could also be physically demanding with long, nighttime marches.

"I earned by Ph.D. at college, but nothing I had done at college was as difficult or intense as training at Camp Ritchie," Stern told the *Catoctin Banner*.

However, Stern could also appreciate the beautiful mountain setting. He enjoyed swimming and canoeing in the lake.

Guy Stern when he returned to the former Fort Ritchie in 2013. Photo is from the author's collection.

The training at Camp Ritchie lasted for three months. His group was then sent to Louisiana for maneuvers that tested whether they had learned the skills they would need in Europe. Stern and other Ritchie Boys were then shipped across the Atlantic. They landed in Birmingham, England.

While in England, the Ritchie Boys took part marginally in the D-Day invasion planning. Stern said that they were in charge of how prisoners captured in the invasion were handled. Once the invasion began, the Ritchie Boys landed three days later to begin their prisoner interrogations.

"Within the first half-hour of being on the beach, we began interrogating people and tinkering with psychological warfare," Stern told the *Record Herald.*

One of their tactics was to play on the fears of German prisoners. When the Ritchie Boys discovered that German soldiers feared being turned over to Russians, Stern began dressing up in the uniform of a Russian officer. Another Ritchie Boy would lead the prisoner into a tent decorated with Russian posters and mementos. Stern would then interrogate the prison in character as a German.

One of Stern's coups was when an Austrian deserter gave him a diary that the deserter had kept from the Battle of the Bulge to his capture at the Rhine River. Stern said that between his interrogations and the diary, he believed the information was correct and useful. It contained details on German morale, plans for troop retreats and hints to the dispersion of other units.

"We could use the information to form the basis of how we directed our propaganda," Stern told the *Catoctin Banner.*

When Stern returned to Camp Ritchie in 2013, he found it very different, at least until sunset. At that time, Lakeside Hall returned to look very much the way it had when it had been an officer's club during World War II.

As part of the Sunset on the Mountain event sponsored by the Fort Ritchie Community Center, the hall was given a period makeover. USO Canteen style food was served and 1940s music played. Sunset on the Mountain also featured an auction with Fort Ritchie and World War II experiences including a ride in an open-cockpit PT-19 trainer aircraft courtesy of the Hagerstown Aviation Museum, a catered dinner at Fort Ritchie's famed Castle, and autographed memorabilia.

Keedysville's Choice Twenty-Five Times

When Charles K. Taylor was elected mayor of Keedysville in 1934, he was just carrying on a family tradition. His grandfather, Christian M. Keedy, was the town's first burgess in 1872. Taylor and his wife, Martha, even lived in a brick house Keedy built in 1874.

Although Taylor had deep roots in Keedysville, he wasn't born there or even in Maryland. He was born in Lacrosse, Kansas, to Charles and Elizabeth Keedy, who later moved to the town.

Since the office of mayor wasn't a full-time job for a town of around 400 at the time, Taylor worked full time as the manager of the Coca-Cola bottling plant in Frederick.

Keedysville history dates back to 1768 when Jacob Hess built a grist mill on the Little Antietam Creek and a house nearby. The mill workers soon built their own log cabins near their work, which became the beginnings of Keedysville, which was originally known as Centerville because of its location halfway between Boonsboro and Sharpsburg.

The Keedy family were among the earliest settlers, and they bought land in the area, including the mill.

As the town grew, a post office was added in 1840. This is when the name of the town changed from Centerville to

Keedysville. The U.S. Postal Department wanted to avoid any confusion with Centerville on the Eastern Shore. Keedysville was chosen in honor of Sammual Keedy, who was the reason the town got its own post office.

The town incorporated in 1872, and Christian Keedy, Taylor's grandfather, was elected burgess, a position equivalent to mayor.

The Taylors showed a strong interest in their community long before Charles became mayor. In 1922, they deeded the town 1.43 acres west of town to be used for athletic purposes. The Works Progress Administration built a baseball field on the property.

Charles was first elected mayor in 1934. He then went on to win election after election each year.

The Keedys donated five acres to the town in 1940 to be used as a public park which the town named Taylor Park.

After a flood of the Little Beaver Creek-Little Antietam Valley caused damaged and contaminated wells in town, Taylor pushed to get the town a public water system. In 1950, Taylor and the town council brought water into Keedysville through lines connected to the Boonsboro water system.

Taylor also served as president of the Frederick County Chamber of Commerce, president of the Frederic Kiwanis Club, president of the Keedysville Homecoming Association, director of the Washington County Red Cress, a member of the Washington County Historical Society, a member of the Mt. Vernon Evangelical and Reformed Church, a member of the Antietam Lodge of the A. F. & A. M., a member of the Olive Branch Chapter of the Order of the Eastern Star, director of the Keedysville Bank, and a member of the McClellan Gun Club.

Taylor died in his home on April 25, 1959, at the age of

61. He had been ill for months, which probably led to him having announced earlier that he wouldn't be running for re-election as mayor for a twenty-sixth term.

"Mr. Taylor was a progressive town official and Keedysville benefitted as a result," the Herald Mail announced.

He passed away in the middle of his 25th consecutive term as mayor. At the time of his death, the *Hagerstown Herald Mail* reported that this was believed to be a county record for most times elected.

It is also one of the longest election streaks in Maryland history. According to the Maryland Municipal League, Harry Knotts of Templeville is the municipal official with the longest-known election streak. Knotts was mayor of Templeville from 1951 to 1952 and then from 1965 to 1995. Like Keedysville, the Templeville mayor's term lasted one year at that time. Also, the current mayor of Templeville, Helen Knotts was recently elected for her twenty-fifth consecutive time, tying Taylor's record.

Taylor is buried in the Fairview Cemetery in Keedysville.

CRIME & PUNISHMENT

Hagerstown Draft Riots

The new U.S. government levied a tax on distilled spirits in 1790 in order to raise revenue. This didn't sit well with farmers who distilled liquor from corn and grain leftover from the harvest. The farmers then sold and traded their liquor for extra income, and they did not want to have to pay a tax on it.

"It was often used as money–a gallon of rye whiskey being equal to a shilling and was widely more acceptable than currency which was not only scarce, but a trifle unstable as well," according to the *Morning Herald.*

Western Pennsylvania residents were particularly vehement in their opposition. Beginning in 1791, various municipalities passed resolutions saying any official who attempted to enforce the tax would be ostracized.

"Collectors were tarred, feathered, whipped, blindfolded and tied in the forests. Once they stripped, burned with a hot iron in a blacksmith shop and then tarred and feathered. A collector's house was broken into and the family terrified and abused," the *Gettysburg Times* reported in 1904.

The violence peaked in July 1794 when citizens attacked the home of tax inspector Gen. John Neville when the U.S. government attempted to serve writs on distillers who hadn't paid the whiskey tax. President George Washington attempted to negotiate with the resisting colonists, but when that failed in early August 1794, he called on governors of states where citizens were rebelling to send militia to control the situation.

Meanwhile, some who favored resisting the government sought to raise support by spreading rumors. "People isolated from eastern governments by distance and illiteracy heard that the excise now included grain–specifically wheat, rye and oats; that plans were afoot to extend the tax to all agricultural products; and that male children were to be excised at fifteen cents and females at ten," Thomas P. Slaughter wrote in *The Whiskey Rebellion.*

Not to be outdone, those who wanted to stir the government to take action against the rebels spread rumors that mobs of men were marching on Frederick Town to take the arsenal there. The rumors placed the numbers in the thousands, although it was closer to 300, and they weren't headed to Frederick Town.

"These reports grossly exaggerated conditions, but where nonetheless relied upon as a basis for decisions," Slaughter wrote.

It created a powder keg that ignited when captains of different companies of soldiers called for volunteers to help put down the rebellion in Western Pennsylvania. Capt. John Schnehley asked for volunteers on behalf of himself and captains Daniel Stull, Robert Douglas, John Geiger, John Lee, and Casper Shaffner.

The men of Washington County not only ignored the draft, they fought back, and several days of rioting started.

"To the cool-headed onlooker was disclosed the fact that the mob was not so prepossessed with the cause at hand as with taking vengeance against any of the private citizens or officials against whom any one of them had a private grudge," according to the *Morning Herald.*

On Sept. 1, the rioters erected a Liberty Pole with "Liberty or Death" written on it in the Market House in Hagerstown. Mostly likely, they also had a cap or hat mounted on the top of them. Liberty poles had been used during the American Revolution and even back to the days of Julius Caesar.

Col. Sprigg and Shryock and Maj. Price tried to stop them by threatening the rebels' lives, but their threats didn't work.

The next day, the liberty pole was gone.

"It was supposed that it was cut down secretly by one of the rioters who had erected it, knowing that the blame would fall on the officials, and thus give the whiskey boys a dubious 'reason' for doing harm to certain prominent citizens," according to the *Morning Herald*.

However, town officials most likely removed it.

This didn't stop the rioters. They mounted a second pole and swore to kill anyone who tried to take it down. They published the threat in a German-language handbill, and also threatened the lives of Washington County Sheriff Adam Ott, Henry Shryock, Rezin Davis, William Lee, Benjamin Clagett, Nathaniel Rochester, and Josiah Price.

"For several days the mob reigned over Hagerstown, enjoying what one account described as a 'complete ascendancy' that local officials were powerless to resist." Slaughter wrote.

Armed citizen patrols took to the street, attempting to restore order.

In Annapolis, Governor Thomas Simm Lee ordered 800 militia, an artillery company, and mounted soldiers to Hagerstown.

They arrived the third week of September and began arresting rioters. They encountered little resistance, and Thomas John Chew Williams wrote in *A History of Washington County, Maryland*, that their courage "was probably of that ephemeral kind which is inspired by whiskey fresh from the stills."

Around 150 people were imprisoned before things calmed down. A schoolteacher was named as the leader of the riot and put on trial.

Six rioters, including the teacher, were marched east to stand trial before the General Court of the Western Shore.

"Prosecutors charged each with waging war against the state, arming himself to that end, and attempting to convince others to join in an assault on law and order. All were acquitted by juries that were unconvinced by the state's eighteen witnesses," Slaughter wrote.

However, the prisoners could have been sentenced to death. This seems to have scared county residents into compliance. One officer remarked that the citizens were "terrified beyond anything he ever saw."

The Unsolved Murder that Haunted Hagerstown

It seems Betty Jane Kennedy of Hagerstown was doomed to lead a short life, but her death continued to haunt Hagerstown for years afterward.

When Betty Jane was just six years old in 1933, a car on West Washington Street hit her. She suffered cuts and a fractured skull. This accident was her fault, though. The police report noted Betty ran out in front of the car, which caused the accident.

She recovered from her injuries, only to suffer a worse fate later.

On April 4, 1946, Martin Benshoff a farmer who lived near the Maryland-Pennsylvania State Line found the body of a young woman laying face down and against a log at the bottom of embankment next to the Waynesboro-Rouzerville Highway in Franklin County, Pa. The woman was also nude except for a pink slip that was twisted around her body and up under her arms.

Benshoff "said he was attracted to the scene when he noticed a woman's faded coat hanging from a tree," reported to the *Hagerstown Daily Mail*. The coat had a store label for Leiter Brothers in it, which gave police a clue to try to identify the woman. A brown leather purse found about a mile away and believed to be the woman's had no identification in it.

The body was taken to Grove Funeral Home in Waynesboro.

The following day, Hagerstown Police, following up on a missing persons report, identified the dead woman as Betty Jane Kennedy, a nineteen-year-old Hagerstown waitress. She had been missing for five days after leaving home following an argument with her older sister.

The body was transported to Hagerstown so the family could arrange funeral services. In the meantime, an autopsy showed Betty Jane had been strangled and her neck was broken. Although she was nude, she had not been raped.

Betty Ann Kennedy.
Taken from a newspaper clipping.

"There was some reason to believe that the victim had been alive when thrown onto the embankment, however," the *Daily Mail* reported.

Washington County Sheriff John B. Huyett said Betty Jane appeared to have been dead twelve to fourteen hours when she was found. This meant she had been murdered during the evening of Apr. 3.

Police in Maryland and Pennsylvania both investigated the case because although Betty Jane had been found in Pennsylvania, it was barely over the state line. Police weren't sure where she had been killed, among other questions.

Betty Jane was last seen alive around 11:30 p.m. the night before her body was found. She left a South Potomac Street restaurant in Hagerstown with a man no one knew. A waitress at the restaurant said he resembled Earl J. McFarland, an escaped killer and rapist from Washington, D.C., who was believed to be in the area.

Police quickly pulled in two men for questioning. One man, who was a taxi driver, who witnesses had seen with Betty Jane the last time she was seen alive. An associate who corroborated the man's alibi said he was working, but the man's boss said he wasn't. Police also discovered the taxi driver had taken a pair of blood-stained pants and a jacket to the dry cleaner the day after Betty Jane's death. Capt. William H. Peters of the Hagerstown Police said these two facts would require a lot of explanation on the taxi driver's part.

A security soldier at Walter Reed who had been AWOL during the time of Betty Jane's death underwent a lie detector test to prove he hadn't been in the area.

By Apr. 12, police had questioned thirty-three people and interviewed hundreds. "Captain Peters said several of the witnesses reversed or changed their stories yesterday when they learned of the possibility of the use of the 'lie detector,' and that fact that the alibis and stories are being changed 'leads us to believe this man knows something about the case,'" the *Daily Mail* reported.

The cabbie said the blood on his jacket and pants was from the bloody nose of a drunk passenger. McFarland, who was never seriously considered a suspect, was captured in Tennessee and had not set foot in Maryland.

By Apr. 15, police were trying to stay optimistic, but the investigation was going nowhere. They did not have a serious suspect, and a lot of unanswered questions remained. Where had Betty Jane spent her nights between the time she left home and the time she died? Where were the rest of her clothes? Where was she killed?

Two weeks after Betty Jane's murder, the Washington County Sheriff offered a $400 reward for information leading to the murderer's arrest and conviction. Of this amount, the sheriff offered $300 from his own pocket because the county commissioners could only offer $100 by law.

Around this time, a woman found a pair of shoes near where Betty Jane's purse was found. Investigators believed the shoes were Betty Jane's.

Police continued investigating, but made no leads or arrests. The lead detective, Carl Hartman, retired in 1948. He said the case was still active, but with his retirement, it went very cold. Nearly 1,000 people had been interviewed or questioned among the seven investigative agencies in two states (FBI, Maryland State Police, Pennsylvania State Police, Hagerstown Police, Washington County Sheriff's Office, Franklin County Sheriff's Office, and Waynesboro Police) with no strong suspects.

Not that there weren't theories about what happened.

One theory said Betty Jane was killed in a hotel because she saw something she shouldn't have. Her body was then lowered through a window to the ground, loaded into a car, and driven away. This theory got a boost when a red dress was discovered during the Potomac Hotel remodeling in 1951. It disappeared by the time the police arrived at the hotel to investigate if it was connected to the murder.

One man confessed to the killing before dying of natural causes, but it turned out he hadn't been in the area at the time of the murder.

"Although Betty Jane wasn't rich, exceptionally beautiful, or murdered in some unusual way, the case became one of the best publicized murders in this area during the 20th century, because of the vast scope of the investigation that followed," the *Daily Mail* reported in 1976.

The murder remains unsolved today.

The Last Person to Suffer a Hanging Offense

On Christmas Eve 1915 around 9 p.m., John Brown approached a small house on a lonely road in Mt. Briar intent on killing.

Susan Dixon, a seventy-six-year-old widow, lived in the home, but Brown believed she was in Shepherdstown, West Virginia, visiting family for the holiday. He was hunting Snook Griffith, Dixon's neighbor who was supposed to be watching her house while she was away. Griffith owed Brown money for work Brown did for him, and Griffith was refusing to pay.

Brown crept around the house, looking through the ground-floor windows until he saw someone sleeping in the bedroom. The bedroom window had a window pane that had been plugged with a rag. Brown carefully removed the rag. Then he poked the shotgun barrel through the window and fired.

The shot missed, destroying the pillow instead.

A person leapt from the bed and hid behind a stove. Brown fired again. This time he hit and killed his target.

Only the dead person wasn't Griffith.

It was Dixon.

In his prison confession, Brown told witnesses, "I don't deny shooting the old woman, but I shot her in mistake for

Snook Griffith."

Dixon's body was found the following day, and as Washington County sheriff's deputies questioned neighbors and friends, they quickly focused their attention on Brown, who witnesses had seen creeping around the house the prior evening. At least one witness heard Brown and Dixon in a heated argument during the day, while another said Dixon had said she was afraid of Brown. Deputies arrested him as he was preparing to board a B&O Railroad car and get out of town.

Police charged Brown with first-degree murder and theft. Dixon had saved twenty dollars toward her eventual burial expenses, and the money, which would be worth about $480 in 2020 dollars, was missing.

After he had been in the county jail a week, Brown told a guard he was ready to tell what happened. The guard called the sheriff and state's attorney, who arrived at the jail to hear the confession.

Besides admitting to killing Dixon, Brown also admitted to taking the missing money, although he said it wasn't on the same night he killed Dixon. As Brown explained it, he visited Dixon a few days before he killed her. He was sitting on her bed talking to her and slipped his hand under the pillow and took the money.

Brown's trial was held in February 1916, and on Mar. 3, the jury found Brown guilty of first-degree murder after deliberating a little over two hours. It was the first conviction of first-degree murder in the county in twelve years.

On a snowy day with a wind blowing that shook the windows of the courtroom, Brown came before Judge Keely and a packed court to hear his sentence. It could be either life in prison or death.

The judge told Brown he had been convicted of first-degree murder and asked him if he had anything to say for himself. Brown didn't.

However, the judge had a lot to say about the case.

He explained why he considered the murder deliberate and not accidental, as Brown claimed. After Brown fired the first shot, which missed Dixon, "you put another shell in your gun, took deliberate aim and shot Mrs. Dixon in the right side of the head and she died," the judge said.

The deliberateness of the act showed he intended to commit murder, even if he had intended the victim to be someone else. Keely went further to say that he believed Brown knew it wasn't Griffith he was trying to kill.

"It is not possible that this poor old woman rose and ran from her bed with no exclamation, as you say," Keely said.

He also did not believe that a woman as poor as Dixon had been who was keeping twenty dollars under her pillow wouldn't have missed it and reported the theft.

Keely said he had looked for reasons to sentence Brown to life in prison rather than death, but he hadn't found it.

"It was a damnable and crying act of bloodshed, inexcusable and unexplainable," Keely said. "There is no possible theory that can exclude this crime from the category of the most deliberate and despicable of murders."

With this pronouncement, he sentenced Brown to hang.

"As the Judge concluded the solemn act, his eyes were wet. He felt it and all felt, everyone more than the man it meant the most to," the *Hagerstown Mail* reported. "There was no demonstration. The prisoner lolled in his seat. No muscle of his face moved."

Deputies took Brown from the courthouse and returned him to the jail. "As Brown was about to enter the jail, whence no more will he emerge alive, he smiled and laughed at some one across the street and waved his arm in farewell and recognition," the *Mail* reported.

Once the judge passed sentence, Sheriff Isaac Long ordered gallows to be made and shipped from Berks County, Pennsylvania. Prisoners in Reading constructed the gallows. It arrived about a week before the scheduled execution and was erected outside of Brown's window.

Hundreds of people wanted to attend the execution, but only people who had been granted tickets were allowed into the jail yard.

On July 7, Brown was awakened early so he could enjoy his final meal. He chose calf heart, crackers, a pickle, and three pints of coffee.

His approaching death hadn't disturbed his sleep the night before. The guards reported he slept well and ate a hearty dinner.

A women's choir and clergy entered the jail to meet with him. The choir sung a variety of hymns including "Nearer My God To Thee," "Son of My Soul," and "Lead Kindly Light." "For an hour while the hymns were softly sung Brown leaned against the bars with downcast eyes," the *Mail* reported. Afterwards, Brown met with the clergy and they gave him whatever reassurances they could.

At 7:40 a.m., the procession filed from the jail into the yard and the crowd that waited there. Sheriff Long led the way, followed by Brown, deputies, clergy, and the women's choir. Flanked by the deputies, Brown mounted the thirteen steps to the top of the gallows.

"As he stepped up onto the fatal platform he looked up at the gallows with a half smile on his face," the *Mail* reported.

The reverend, who was the sheriff's son, offered a prayer. Sheriff Long asked Brown if he had any final words. Brown didn't.

The sheriff patted Brown's legs to move him over the trap door. A black cap was placed over his head, and his hands were handcuffed behind him. A deputy then placed the noose around Brown's neck.

The sheriff walked down a step and jerked a rope that triggered the trap door to open at 7:54 a.m. There was a loud thump as the body dropped, but Brown did not kick.

His neck did not break in the drop. A doctor checked the body after a few minutes and still detected a heartbeat. The doctor finally declared Brown dead at 8:16 a.m.

This was only the third hanging Washington County had had since 1863.

Brown's body was removed and buried in Bellevue Graveyard at county expense.

After the hanging, the gallows were dismantled in case they were needed again.

They weren't.

"Since Brown, the only living creatures that have hung from it have been spiders in summer cobwebs," the *Daily Mail* reported in 1972.

However, in the mid-1960s, it was reassembled in the jail yard and displayed for years. It was finally removed after people kept complaining that it was inappropriate to keep on display.

Making Mountain Dew, White Lightning, Hooch, Moonshine

When the federal government banned the sale, production, and transportation of alcohol in the United States in 1919, citizens had to choose between becoming teetotalers or criminals. Many law-abiding citizens chose the latter.

Since a person could get in trouble buying a drink, people who did it didn't talk about it. That didn't mean that it wasn't happening. Underground bars, or speakeasies, weren't advertised. People knew about them by word of mouth. You got in by knowing someone or knowing a password. Manufacturing moved to stills hidden in the woods or basements.

Moonshining (the illegal manufacture or distribution of alcohol) has been around since the Whiskey Rebellion in the 1790s. The Western Pennsylvanians who refused to pay the federal taxes on homemade liquor were the country's first moonshiners.

However, it wasn't until the Prohibition era that moonshining took off because the demand for alcohol increased. With the profits rising—a quart of moonshine could fetch $16 ($225 in today's dollars) in Hagerstown, Md.—, more and more people were willing to risk being arrested and became moonshiners, rumrunners, bootleggers.

Moonshining in Pen Mar

Pen Mar Park, with its ideal location as a resort on the border between Maryland and Pennsylvania, became a favorite spot for bootleggers to hide their stills. Also, being at Pen Mar put them close to people who wanted to relax and enjoy themselves with a drink. In 1921, an informant told police that there were thirteen stills that he knew of near Pen Mar. The bootleggers were making a lot of money selling their product, though they didn't stay long in one place.

Blue Mountain House at Pen Mar was a popular tourist destination during Prohibition, which meant local bootleggers had a large customer base. Photo courtesy of the Library of Congress.

The *Gettysburg Compiler* reported that one informant about the bootlegging at Pen Mar saw "a bootlegger with a suitcase, placed the latter on a rock near the old Blue Mountain House path and did a land office business by handing the liquor out by the pint and half pint to people who appeared from among the bushes."

After a few minutes, he closed up shop, disappeared into the woods only to reappear in another location about half an hour later.

In 1925 revenuers tried to get Daniel Toms' 30-gallon still in Cascade. He held them off for a short time with a shotgun, but they eventually surrounded him and caught him and his henchmen.

Smithsburg Moonshining War

Revenuers also spent plenty of time in Smithsburg combing the hills for moonshiners. They tried to pass themselves off as tourist hikers.

Smithsburg also made national headlines as having an "old-time mountain feud" between John Cline and Henry Russman involving night raiding, indiscriminate shooting, and fights. They were accused of wrecking a church, dynamiting a sawmill, killing one person, and wounding others. A 1923 article estimated that there were 500 stills between Hagerstown and the Pennsylvania line. The interest in this fighting may have been due in part to the recent coal mine riots that had grown so violent across the country.

"They are unmolested. It would be as much as an officer's life would be worth to try and interfere. The natives are silent. They know a bullet in the dark would follow any giving of information," the *Hagerstown Mail* reported.

Thurmont Moonshining

Former Catoctin Mountain Park Ranger Debra Mills explained that Catoctin Mountain was much more barren during the Prohibition era and the people who lived on it were impoverished.

"Prohibition was probably a good thing economically for people in this area," Mills said.

Having stills operating nearby gave farmers a place to sell their crops. Although corn was the most popular grain for moonshine, Elmer Black of Thurmont said in a 2015 interview that he only ever knew of rye being raised to sell to the local moonshiners in the area.

The remnants of a still on Catoctin Mountain. Photo courtesy of the Catoctin Mountain Park photo archives.

The finished product was often shipped out of the area on the railroad in barrels labeled cornmeal, according to Mills.

It could leave other ways as well. Black recalled that his grandfather would often run moonshine right under the nose of the county sheriff and his deputies. He would get the family together to take a ride in their Studebaker and off they would go. There was an ulterior motive for the drive, though. He had hidden moonshine underneath the seats.

"My grandfather would wave 'hi' as they went by the sheriff," Black said.

Two of Black's uncles were some of the most-successful bootleggers around the Thurmont, Md., area. Even his father was known to drive moonshine out of the region to sell. One time he took Black and his sibling along for the ride. The kids fell asleep.

"The three of us woke up and asked who lives here," Black said. "Some senator they told us. They were rolling the barrels up to the house."

They were hidden on the mountain near streams that could supply them with the water needed for the moonshine recipes. According to Black, if you follow the streams on Catoctin Mountain upriver, you can still see the remnants of destroyed stills.

Martin shared some of his family stories during a presentation at the Thurmont Regional Library in 2016 about moonshining.

One grandfather kept a quarter keg of moonshine in his attic, and when friends would come by with Mason jars, Martin's grandfather would tell his son to go up and get some 'shine for the friends.

At some point, Martin's grandfather moved the keg from the attic to the basement and buried it in the coal pile.

Once, revenue agents came by wanting to search the house while Martin's father was alone. The boy didn't know what to do because he couldn't get on the phone to call his parents, so he let the revenue agents in to search the house.

They started in the attic which worried Martin's father, but the men found nothing. Martin's father thought he was safe and that the moonshine was no longer in the house. The revenue agents continued their search, ending up in the basement.

One agent saw the coal pile and wondered if moonshine might be buried in it. Martin's father, not knowing that was the case, held up the coal shovel and told the agents, "Go ahead and dig, but you've got to put it all back, or my dad will be mad."

Luckily, the agents were lazy and chose not to dig. Martin's grandfather moved the moonshine out of the house after that.

The revenue agents did eventually catch up with Martin's grandfather. According to Martin, they came in the front door of the house chasing Martin's grandfather while the man went out the back door. The federal agents chased after him.

Martin's father, a young boy at the time, chased after the men. "Dad, he caught up with one revenuer and bit him on the leg and my grandfather got away," Martin said.

End of an era

Due to its unpopularity, Prohibition soon ended after the election of Franklin D. Roosevelt in 1932. Everyone went out and drank to his health.

Monsters and Mayhem

The Hunt for the Snallygaster

Scotland has Nessie, and the American Northwest has Bigfoot. They are legendary monsters. Washington and Frederick counties have their own monster called the snallygaster.

People in Marylanders have reported snallygasters for centuries. Some people believe the name has German origins. "Schnelle geist" means "fast ghost."

Initially, snallygasters were reptilian birds that preyed on poultry and children.

Western Maryland's snallygaster is decidedly nastier.

On February 12, 1909, folks around Middletown opened their newspapers to read that a large winged creature had swooped down and carried off a man walking along the road. The beast then sucked out most of the man's blood and tossed the empty carcass aside.

"And either the folks in Western Maryland were unusually impressionable or there really was something terrible on the loose, because within hours of the first appearance in the Register, people in Frederick and Washington Counties and even nearby Shepherdstown, West Virginia, began reporting encounters with the flying monster," Susan Fair wrote in *Legends and Lore of Western Maryland*. A man from Casstown, Ohio, wrote in the same issue and called the creature a snallygaster.

Descriptions vary, but once you saw it, you would definitely remember it. Dragonlike, long wings, long pointed tail, sometimes with a horn, one eye in the middle of its forehead, octopus-like tentacles that trailed behind like streamers, retractable claws. Some reports noted that the claws were razor sharp. One woman said the snallygaster had hoofs. A man named George Jacobs said he shot at the snallygaster while hunting. Fair wrote, "…the monster apparently didn't care for being shot at. As a matter of fact, it was so annoyed that it pursued Jacobs across a field, all the while lunging angrily—or perhaps hungrily—at the terrified man's neck."

The *Hagerstown Mail* said that the Smithsonian Institution wanted to examine the creature. The *Middletown Valley Register* reported that the military was sending in soldiers armed with Gatling guns.

President Theodore Roosevelt was said to be considering a big-game hunt in Africa to stalk an even greater prize in the snallygaster.

People around Middletown were terrified. Harry Wachtel of Myersville shot and wounded what he thought was the snallygaster.

It turned out to be a large owl.

"Some say it is a Canadian owl, some say it is just a 'booby owl,' but all agree that with its weird gray wings spread in the cold dead of night it would be taken for a 'snallygaster,' 'jabberwock,' 'wampdoodle' or another terrifying species," the *Frederick Post* reported.

The snallygaster appeared throughout the Middletown Valley, on South Mountain, on Catoctin Mountain, and even as far west as Cumberland, Md., where the snallygaster spoke for the first time.

It reportedly attacked a man there and said, "My, I'm dry! I haven't had a good drink since I was killed in the Battle of Chickamauga." With that report, people started wondering if the creature was a reincarnated Civil War soldier.

In Sharpsburg, it was reported the nest of eggs from the creature was found.

An artist's depiction of the snallygaster.
Courtesy of Wikimedia Commons.

In Emmitsburg, the creature supposedly tried to grab Ed Brown, a worker on the Emmitsburg Railroad. The beast caught him, but lucky for Brown, his suspender snapped, and he got away. A mob pursued the snallygaster, which then displayed a new skill—shooting fire from its nostrils.

This was the last sighting of the snallygaster for 23 years. In November 1932, reports of the snallygaster began again and even received some national attention. This time, there weren't reports of attacks, but people were scared just the same.

A Canadian owl which was mistaken for the snallygaster once, and may have actually been the source of the stories. Photo courtesy of Wikimedia Commons.

On Dec. 21, the *Hagerstown Morning Herald* ran the headline: "Death of Snallygaster is reported: Accounts Differ." The newspaper article stated, "The snallygaster circled for sometime above a 2,500-gallon vat, apparently attracted by the fumes. Finally, however, the fumes became too strong, and the creature fell directly into the mash."

A revenue agent and Washington County deputy were supposedly raiding the still around the same time and found the monster, not the bootleggers, who had fled at the sight of the snallygaster.

George Danforth, the revenue agent, was quoted as saying, "Imagine our feeling when our eyes feasted on the monster submerged in the liquor vat."

Apparently, lye in the mash vat supposedly ate away the snallygaster's flesh.

"The remains of the snallygaster were lost to science when Danforth—carrying out his prohibition duties—order the vat and contents destroyed with a large charge of dynamite," the *Cumberland Evening Times* reported.

A few years after the snallygaster's death, another one was reportedly seen in the Middletown Valley area. This one was smaller, though.

"Those who believe that the young monster is a small snallygaster, claim that the unusual heat of the present summer caused one of the eggs to hatch prematurely," the *Hagerstown Daily Mail* reported.

The article also noted scientists claimed it took fifteen to twenty years for snallygaster eggs to hatch, so if the new snallygaster was an offspring of the one that had died in the moonshine vat, its offspring weren't expected to put in an appearance until 1949 at the earliest.

And so, the legend of the snallygaster continued.

Fair suggests that the story of the snallygaster was inspired by stories of a similar creature called the Jersey Devil. The snallygaster put in its appearance shortly after that.

Some thought the creature was created to scare hobos and vagabonds from Middletown.

Thomas Harbaugh was the Ohio man who first referenced the snallygaster. He was a native of Middletown, though. He was also the author of 650 "nickel novels." He was also good friends with the *Register* editor, George Rhoderick.

"All it took was one little story, and local residents—not to mention reporters and editors of competing newspapers—were ready to release their inner monsters, collaborating on a creation that gleefully took on a life of its own," Fair suggested.

The snallygaster's attack on livestock in Middletown Valley. Courtesy of Wikimedia Commons.

Western Maryland's Earthquake Capital

No one can say Maryland is earthquake prone. Over 244 years from 1758 to 2002, only sixty-one earthquakes were reported in the state. That's roughly one earthquake every four years, and they weren't severe. In fact, nearly all of them measured under 3.0 on the Richter scale. Maryland has felt larger earthquakes, but they originated outside of the state.

Looking at a map of these earthquakes, west of Carroll County tends to be an earthquake-free zone in Maryland, except for two small quakes. Both occurred near Hancock.

The first Hancock earthquake happened on September 7, 1962, at 2 p.m. It started about 38 kilometers beneath the surface and registered 3.3 on the Richter Scale for magnitude. It also measured 4 out of 12 for intensity on the Modified Mercalli Intensity Scale (a subjective scale that relies on witness accounts). It apparently was not a significant disturbance because even though a picture of an Iranian earthquake victim ran in the newspapers, no mention was made of the Hancock earthquake.

The second earthquake occurred at 7:30 p.m. on April 26, 1978. It started about 15 kilometers below the surface and registered. 3.10 on the Richter Scale. According to the U.S. Geological Survey this is the strongest Maryland earthquake on official record, but this does not include quakes that predate the U.S. Geological Survey's measurements. While some Maryland earthquakes may have been stronger, the severity can only be estimated by reports from the time.

Although both Hancock earthquakes are considered mild (for comparison, the famous 1903 San Francisco Earthquake registered 8.3 on the Richter Scale), these quakes were among the worst earthquakes in the state, and they are likely to remain so. However, Homefacts.com estimates the county's chance of a 5.0 earthquake in the next 50 years at .84 percent.

"Very little is known about the causes of earthquakes in the eastern United States. In general, there is no clear association among seismicity, geologic structure, and surface displacement, in contrast to a common association in the western U.S.," James Reger wrote in his article, "Earthquakes and MD."

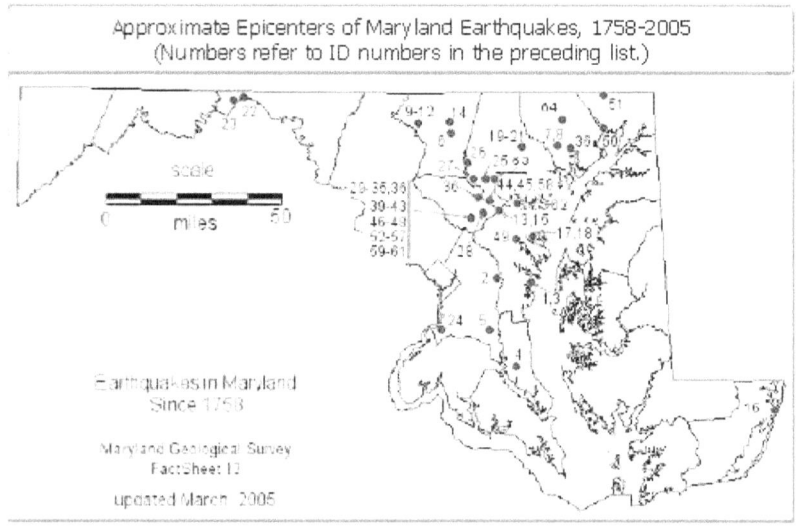

The Maryland Geological Survey's map of Maryland earthquakes.

Although Maryland has faults (cracks where earthquakes tend to occur), none of them are believed to be active.

"The mid-Atlantic and central Appalachian region, including Maryland, is characterized by a moderate amount of low-level earthquake activity, but their cause or causes are largely a matter of speculation. In Maryland, for example, there are numerous faults, but none is known or suspected to be active. Because of the relatively low seismic energy release, this region has received relatively little attention from earthquake seismologists (Bollinger, 1969)," according to the Maryland Geological Survey.

Columbia is the most active area in Maryland for earthquakes, home to more than a third of state's earthquakes. The quakes also appear to stay in one area for a time before moving on. For instance, no other event occurred in Maryland durin the sixteen years between the Hancock quakes. Union Bridge had four earthquakes over two years with no other quakes in the state between. Phoenix and Columbia each had three earthquakes in one year.

"Our earthquakes typically come in swarms. There will be two or three during the course of a week or two, and then it will be quiet for a few years," said Richard Ortt, director and state geologist, Maryland Geological Survey.

"The last earthquake to cause appreciable damage in the eastern United States occurred in 1886 near Charleston, South Carolina. It had an estimated magnitude of 6.5-7, an intensity of X, and was felt over an area of two million square miles. Even in Maryland, the felt intensity from this earthquake was IV to V," Reger wrote.

The most damaging earthquake experienced in Maryland actually took place in Virginia, South Carolina and Missouri.

Maryland has two seismometers monitoring for earthquake activity. One was installed in 2000 at Soldiers Delight Natural Environmental Area in Baltimore County, and the other is located in Garrett County and was installed in 2018.

The Flood to End All Floods

People knew the flood was coming. A warm spell in the middle of March 1936 started the heavy snowpack in the Western Maryland mountains melting.

"There was snow in the mountains. I forget how many inches was up there. Cold and freezing up to that time," Maurice Snyder said in a 2011 interview on *Whilbr.org*. Snyder lived through the flood. "Couple of days prior to that a warm spell came in, some rain and it began to melt and the harder it started to melt up in Cumberland it started coming down the river and calls went out for low lands to get ready to move out."

Stories quickly rising water raced eastward down the river, and the residents of Hancock, Williamsport, and other riverside communities knew the trouble was heading in their direction.

The front page headline on the *Hagerstown Daily Mail* declared, "New Potomac Flood Looms; River Rises."

And Potomac River did rise… quickly. The *Daily Mail* reported, for a time, the river rose 19 inches an hour. At Williamsport, the river ran a half mile wide, twice its normal width.

"Warnings of the wall of water that could be expected during the night sent scores of families there scurrying to higher ground early last night and they abandoned their homes in the nick of time, for an unprecedented rise came during the night," the *Daily Mail* reported.

The flood hits

The Potomac Edison plant near Williamsport flooded and shut down, leaving Williamsport and other areas of the county without power. Williamsport was without power for more than a day. Floodwaters swept the Kelly Sawmill near Dam No. 4 and 5,000 feet of lumber into the river along with tools, crossties, and gasoline in drums.

The Cushwa's warehouse underwater during the 1936 Potomac River flood. Photo courtesy of Whilbr.org.

"River freighted with small buildings, trees and all kinds of debris with probably a hundred buildings in and around Williamsport swept away," the *Cumberland Evening Times* reported.

The Potomac Boat Club clubhouses and a hay building near the Cushwa warehouse also disappeared into the river.

"Clubhouses and residences apparently have been hard hit from Hancock to Harper's Ferry, for several buildings were seen floating down the Potomac at Williamsport this morning," the *Daily Mail* reported.

One building washed into the river and up against the piers of the bridge over the Potomac at Williamsport. As hundreds of people watched, the water batter it to pieces against the piers, and the debris continued its journey down the river.

Rowing down Main Street in Hancock during the 1936 flood. Photo courtesy of Whilbr.org.

The *Morning Herald* reported, "The town of Williamsport resembled a small community on fair day. The community was literally packed and jammed with visitors. More than 4,000 people paid ten cents to view the surging waters from the big bridge. They saw a wide, muddy stream rolling headlong carrying with it debris of all kinds; they say submerged houses, trees and boxcars. It was truly an awe-inspiring spectacle."

Jack Myers lived next to Cushwa's brick yard in 1936. He was interviewed in 2011, which is available on *Whilbr.org*. Myers said, "...we were almost surrounded by water. I can still hear the, you know the brickyard had what we called kilns where they burnt their bricks and they burnt the clay to make bricks. Well, the flood came up and hit that fire, it was hot, the kilns were hot, and it is hard to describe what that sounded like, you know. The steam came up and there was a kind of muffled sound – it was amazing. I can still remember that."

The Potomac Edison power plant flooded and had to shut down during the 1936 flood. Photo courtesy of Whilbr.org.

He and his father were moving furniture from the first floor to the second when Myers' father decided it was time for them to get to higher ground. They got in a motorboat they owned and headed into Williamsport.

"Like I said, the only way we knowed where to go, we followed the tops of the telephone poles, because the bridge was completely covered over." Myers said. "And when we docked over there in Williamsport it was at Joe Grove's barber shop, half way up what we called town hill."

The pumping station for the Hagerstown water system shut down, leaving Hagerstown without much of the water the city needed.

People called the police and fire companies for help, but the problem was reaching them. National Highway was impassable at Hancock, as the newspapermen trying to go west to see the flood damage in Cumberland discovered.

The Potomac River eventually crested at 49.5 feet at Williamsport, 5 feet higher than the 1889 flood. Other communities along the river saw similarly high crests, making this the worst flood the Potomac River has ever experienced.

In Hancock, Main Street flooded to a depth of 15 feet at times, and the town could only be reached by boat. The railroad tracks and roads were all under water. Battered by water and debris, part of the bridge across the Potomac also collapsed. Before it fell, it was underwater, and it sat 65 feet above the river normally.

"(Joseph) Wolfe said families could reach the second floors of their flood homes by boat," the *Cumberland Evening Times* reported from a town resident.

Three hundred of the 945 people in town were left homeless during the flood. A dozen homes washed away in the flooding and even more were damaged.

The *Hancock News* staff worked during the flood to get out the newspaper. Meanwhile, the first floor of their building filled with water. The newspaper reported floodwaters throughout the town ranged from half a food deep to 25 feet deep. "It was a common, yet distressing sight to see buildings torn from their moorings, floating about like tops," the newspaper reported.

WPA workers were recruited to help families evacuate their flooded homes. Maryland State Police and other local police helped manage traffic in the affected areas of the county.

Hancock's Main Street near the intersection with Pennsylvania Avenue. Photo courtesy of Whilbr.org.

The aftermath

Hancock was the second-hardest-hit community along the Potomac River. The flood did an estimated $250,000 ($4.7 million in 2021 dollars) damage to the town. Only Cumberland fared worse.

Dr. H. E. Tabler, chairman of the State Roads Commission, estimated the damage to state highways and property in Western Maryland to be nearly $900,000 ($17.1 million in 2021 dollars) with $188,000 ($3.6 million in 2021 dollars) in Washington County.

Washington County officials estimated it would take $15,000 ($285,000 in 2021 dollars) to repair and clean debris from damaged homes and the same amount to get the Hagerstown Water Department pumping station operating again.

A report to the Maryland Legislature near the end of March 1936 found the flood had damaged 2,216 Maryland homes in five counties. The majority of these homes was in Allegany County (1,800). In Washington County, 261 homes were damaged or lost, including 76 in Hancock and 60 in Williamsport.

Once the waters receded back within the banks of the Potomac River, the cleanup began.

"There was mud all over the floor, all over everything. Just think about that, mud up on the second floor, everywhere. That all had to be shoveled out and washed down. You had to re-wallpaper, and repaint. And you know what water does to wood. There would be lots of swelling and repairs to be made. I remember working on the houses to clean them up, to try to get them cleaned up," Myers said.

The Washington County Health Department chlorinated wells to make the water drinkable and provided line for flooded basements. They also offered inoculations against typhoid which was a worry in the aftermath of the flood since many water sources were contaminated.

"Dr. Cameron, I think that was his name, they were afraid of a typhoid epidemic or something," Snyder said. "He was closing the factories, he closed the tannery and gave everyone a shot for typhoid, at that time. He tried to protect the health end of it. He started over there, I think Cushwa's got it, the tannery got it, anybody on the streets if they could get them. They were giving them the shots to protect the health in them."

Workers with the Department of Natural Resources started seineing the canal to rescue any fish trapped there. However, fish turned up in some unusual places. One canal lock-keeper returned to his house to find seven sucker fish flopping around on the second floor of his lockhouse.

While the Potomac River was hard hit in the flood, just about every river in the Mid-Atlantic region seems to have flooded in the storm system. The estimated dead in the flooding ranges from 150 to 177, depending on the source. Nobody in Washington County was reported killed in the flooding.

The Hancock bridge over the Potomac is partially underwater during the 1936 flood. Photo courtesy of Whilbr.org.

Washington County's Deadliest Killer

In the fall of 1918, as Allied forces swept across Europe to victory, a new war was beginning that would kill five percent of the world's population in less than a year. Spanish Flu struck quickly, and it reached just about everywhere around the globe, including Washington County where it left thousands of residents sick and hundreds of people dead.

"It was a perfect storm of events that made Spanish Flu so bad," says Diana Gaviria, medical director with the Washington County Health Department.

It has also left researchers worried that after 100 years, the world may be due for another pandemic.

"There's a lot of research going on even now as to why it was so deadly," said Gaviria.

Researchers have gone so far as to take samples from people who died from the 1918 flu pandemic and reconstruct the virus to study it. And because researchers still aren't sure why it was so deadly or how to combat that particular flu strain, Gaviria says that the reconstructed samples are treated like "high-level, biological weapons."

Spanish Flu in Washington County

Spanish Flu killed more people than World War I and in

a shorter time frame, too, yet the war had the headlines during 1918 because it was winding down at the same time the Spanish Flu was reaching its peak. Deadlier than the Black Plague, Spanish Flu was so devastating that human lifespan was reduced by ten years in 1918.

Police officers wearing face masks during the Spanish Flu pandemic. Photo courtesy of the Library of Congress.

Its lethality wasn't apparent at first, and few people saw the flu as a threat. They knew they and their friends were getting sick, but they just figured it was a seasonal flu. Newspapers downplayed the effects of the flu or ignored it completely.

The *Morning Herald* and *Daily Mail* finally began to notice the flu on Oct. 5. Most likely, this was because the day before, Pennsylvania had enacted a drastic order that shut down most public meeting places in the state. (Maryland took similar actions on Oct. 8.)

Soon stories of the flu appeared daily in the newspaper. In an unusual case, Brent Gilbert Smith, a forty-seven-year-old family man in Hancock, shot himself in the temple, apparently in a delirium brought on by the flu.

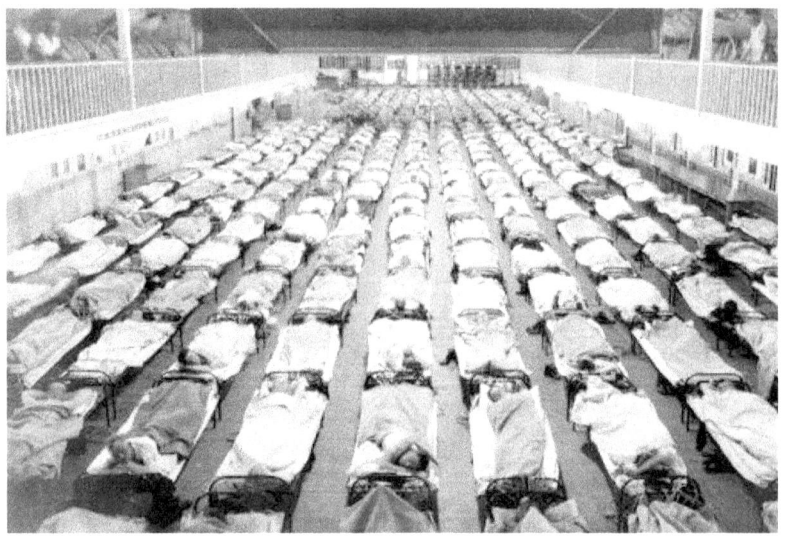

An emergency hospital in Kansas during the Spanish Flu pandemic. Photo courtesy of the Library of Congress.

Big Pool was noted as particularly bad where the flu had hit, "Only one family in the Big Pool section has so far escaped and in some instances entire families are down," the *Morning Herald* reported.

One case on Oct. 9 shows how quickly the flu could strike. Conductor M. Thompson left his home on Franklin Street to go to the Elizabeth Street railroad office. Just as he reached the office, he fell over ill. It is reported he was taken with the flu from the time he left home, only a short time before. It took four men to carry him into the yard office. Later he was sent home.

Doctors were overtaxed as they were called both day and

night. The *Morning Herald* reported, "It is a common thing for whole families to be down and local physicians who are not afflicted themselves, are unable to see all of their patients as they would like and are compelled to have them wait, which is a condition not at all desirable but which cannot be helped under the stressing situation."

The county fair was reluctantly canceled that year, and emergency hospitals were opened. The country club was turned into a hospital run by Dr. Dunott, and the Western Maryland Railroad had a traveling emergency hospital that moved through communities along the line.

The Red Cross set up a Victory Kitchen that served meals to families who were too sick to care for themselves. They also set up an emergency nursery in the mansion house in the city park. Families whose parents were too sick to care for their children had their youngsters cared for in the emergency nursery.

By this time, the flu had not only spread wildly throughout the county, but deaths were increasing. On Oct. 20, 15 people died from the flu. Their ages ranged from nineteen to sixty-eight.

The *Morning Herald* reported that about forty people died in Washington County during a typical month. However, between Oct. 14-18, thirty-one people died, and although the final numbers for the previous weekend hadn't been reported at that time, it appeared that each day was going to be worse than any other day that season. This would have put the deaths from just the second week of October at around sixty-five.

Although firm cumulative numbers for the county aren't available, an estimated 6,000 people caught the flu, based on reported deaths and the death rates in surrounding counties, 400 people died.

Gaviria said, that what was really dramatic about the Spanish flu was the high fatality rate among typically healthy young people with robust immune systems.

Protecting yourself from the flu today

Influenza or flu is an infection of the nose, throat, and lungs caused by the influenza virus. The virus spreads through the air when people cough. It can also spread by direct contact with an infected person. Symptoms — which tend to begin one to four days after a person is infected — might include chills, fever, coughing, headaches, muscle aches, sore throat, runny nose, and fatigue. Although not considered a deadly disease, common seasonal flu can lead to serious complications like pneumonia, bronchitis, high fever and, in children, seizures. According to the Centers for Disease Control and Prevention, flu-related complications kill about 36,000 people, mostly the elderly, each year in the United States.

As with many other localities, Washington County has an emergency preparedness plan that can be enacted in the event of a pandemic situation. The plan involves anti-viral medications, supportive treatment, and preventative measures.

"Our level of response and when it starts depends on how widespread the outbreak would be," said Gaviria.

She added that the county is prepared for mass distribution and mass vaccinations should the need arise. However, this might lag a few months behind the outbreak of a new flu strain because of the time needed to produce a vaccine.

Gaviria also said that health agencies are always watching for novel strains of the flu that might signal a particularly virulent or deadly version of the flu.

She said, "Last year was a severe season, probably the worse since the H1N1 outbreak in 2009-2010."

Prevention

Preventing the flu essentially boils down to not coming in contact with the virus. In addition to avoiding contact with infected individuals, one of the best ways to avoid getting sick is to wash your hands thoroughly.

Face masks were required on public transportation during the Spanish Flu pandemic. Photo courtesy of the Library of Congress.

Vaccinations also reduce the likelihood of catching the flu and are recommended for those with weaker immune systems — especially children and the elderly.

"You cannot get the flu from flu shots," Gaviria said. "They use either a piece of deactivated virus or a deactivated virus. It is biologically impossible for you to get the flu from a shot."

Because the flu virus can mutate rapidly, new vaccines are developed and administered each year to combat the newest strains. A vaccine's effectiveness depends on how little the flu has changed over the year.

Also, show some concern for those around you, so you don't pass on the flu. Cough into your sleeve, and stay home when you are sick.

ODDS & ENDS

Amphibian Love Made Hagerstown Famous

In 1932, Charles Clyde (C. C.) Moler was shopping at Lilypons goldfish nurseries in Frederick County when something in the water caught his eye. The water rippled with activity from the thousands of goldfish in the ponds that been drained to a low level for harvesting. C. C. saw flashes of orange from the goldfish and greenish brown from tadpoles that shared the ponds, but he saw something else, too.

An occasional flash of white caught his eye. He looked closer and saw it was a tadpole. Lilypons raised tadpoles as well as goldfish. Tadpoles acted as scavengers in a goldfish aquarium, eating any food the fish didn't and helping keep the tank clean.

C. C. pointed out the white tadpoles and had a worker fish them out. He found three. Each one was white with pink eyes. They were albino, a rare congenital defect that causes the loss of any pigmentation.

When asked about an albino frog in the New York Museum of History's collection at the time, herpetologist Dr. Raymond Ditmars called it, "rarer than human quintuplets." C. C. had hit a biological lottery jackpot.

"At that time the museum's specimen was thought to be the only one in existence and, although widespread publicity brought to light several others, the white frog still holds his rank as one of the rarest forms of albinism," The *Baltimore Sun* reported.

Moler surprised Lilypons workers when he told them how rare albino frogs were. They had first noticed albino tadpoles in their ponds the previous year. "No special thought was given to their unusual appearance and, after passing through the regular grading process, a few were shipped out with the normal tadpoles. Several dealers complained that they had received tadpoles which were apparently sick, but no one realized that a rare find had been passed by so casually," *The Baltimore Sun* reported.

Moler had Lilypons tried to trace the albino tadpoles that had been shipped out. Of the ones they found, "only one had lived to frogdom, and that was dead and resting in alcohol," according to *The Sun*.

With the news of the rare find, other goldfish farmers in Frederick County started watching the tadpoles they harvested from their ponds. No other ponds yielded the rare albino frogs.

Moler kept the three he found and returned home to Hagerstown. Two of the tadpoles died, but one matured to an albino male bullfrog.

Moler worked as an electrical engineer for Potomac Edison, but caring for the albino frog became his hobby.

He returned to Lilypons the following year during their harvest and found more white tadpoles that he purchased. With a year's experience, he was better able to care for them. Their tanks were temperature controlled to be no lower than sixty-five degrees. Moler fed them only live food, primarily earthworms, because frogs won't eat anything that doesn't move.

One of these tadpoles matured to a female of the same species as the male.

"Today they dwell happily together, the world's first pair of albino frogs, and it is hoped that they will be the Adam and Eve of a new race," *The Sun* reported. They were believed to be the only breeding pair of albino bullfrogs in the world.

Experts gave Moler a 50-50 chance of being able to breed them, but he beat the odds and the *Hagerstown Morning Herald* reported in 1937, he had "several hundred Albino tadpoles as a reward." Of these, he hoped to get as many as 200 to grow to adulthood, but only twenty-three did.

The sign in front of C. C. Moler's white frog farm. Photo courtesy of the Library of Congress.

C. C. was so pleased with his success he presented a pair of albino frogs to the New York Museum of Natural History as a gift. In accepting the gift, Museum Director Dr. G. Kingsley Noble said, "You have already made a very important contribution to science in successfully rearing these delicate creatures."

The *New York Times* called Moler, "the world's only collector and breeder of Albino frogs."

With his collection of albino frogs growing, Moler purchased a farm near Wagner's Crossroad on Beaver Creek, along the new Dual Highway. He had three screened outdoor pools built on the property. He then purchased three abandoned Hagerstown and Frederick Railway trolley cars and placed one next to each pool. C. C. converted one trolley into a massive heated aquarium where the tadpoles could stay in the winter. Other tadpoles were left in the pools where they disappeared into the mud at the bottom. Moler wanted to see if the albino frogs could survive the winter as well as regular frogs.

The farm soon became a tourist attraction advertising itself as having the only white frog colony in the world.

Moler kept the farm going until he retired in 1953.

Hagerstown's Blues, Terriers, Champs, & Hubs

On Wednesday morning, May 19, 1915, fourteen young, energetic men walked and jogged from the Franklin Hotel in Hagerstown to the Athletic Park. "Their suits tattered and torn beyond description and a bewildering array of every conceivable color and style the try-outers presented a sorrowful appearance and gave the innocent and unsophisticated onlookers the impressions that they had been in a wreck or happened with something decidedly terrible," the *Hagerstown Morning Herald* reported.

This ragtag group of players was the beginning of professional baseball in the Washington County. About 100 onlookers turned out at the park to watch these young men practice and prove themselves worthy to be called professional baseball players in the new Blue Ridge Professional Baseball League.

Beginnings

Charles Boyer had moved back to the Hagerstown area from the South in 1914. He owned several theaters, but he also loved baseball. He was the former president of the South Atlantic Baseball League, a Class C professional baseball league that operated from 1904 to 1917.

In Hagerstown, he saw town teams playing against each

other and saw that the talent among the players. He purchased the Hagerstown team and set to work forming the Blue Ridge League.

Once Boyer had created an interest in the league and had teams wanting to join, he applied to the National Baseball Commission. In March 1915, Commission President John Tener designated the Blue Ridge League as a Class D league, the lowest level of professional baseball at the time.

Charles W. Boyer, the Hagerstown businessman who formed the Blue Ridge League. Photo courtesy of Robert Savitt.

"It was entry level baseball," Robert Savitt, author of *The Blue Ridge League* said. "Even though the players got paid, they still needed to have other jobs."

As the teams set about recruiting players, they had little

to offer, despite the fact they were professional teams. The players would be paid, even if it was a pittance, and they would be recognized as professional players.

Each team could have no more than 13 players, which included the required player-manager. The total monthly salary cap was $1,300 a month. Some clubs didn't even have a cap that high.

By the time that the league was ready for its inaugural season, six teams from Chambersburg, Frederick, Gettysburg, Hagerstown, Hanover, and Martinsburg made up the Blue Ridge League.

Opening day

Opening day in Washington County started off with a parade through town at 2 p.m. followed by a 3 p.m. game on Friday, May 28, 1915. The *Morning Herald* reported, "When the umpire shouts, 'Play ball!' at Willow Lane Park promptly at 3 o'clock this afternoon, the biggest crowd ever seen at a ball game in Hagerstown is expected to pack the new grandstand, bleachers, fences and standing room."

The parade comprised a marching band followed by a creeping line of cars with players waving to fans. Some businesses closed at noon, so their employees could attend the game. In some cases, the employers had no choice. One man mentioned in the newspaper said he had closed up because all of his workmen asked off.

One female fan said, "I waited six hours in New York to see a world's championship game and I am going to see the game this afternoon if I have to crawl through a knothole in the fence."

An estimated 2,000 people showed up to watch the game. The Mayor of Hagerstown threw out the first pitch. The game itself was tightly played with only seven hits. The

Hagerstown Blues won 3-1.

By mid-August 1915, the Frederick Hustlers had clinched the first pennant for the Blue Ridge League with six scheduled games left. The *Frederick Daily News* reported, "They have obtained such a lead in the last month that it will not be necessary to play off the several postponed and tie games." The team finished the season with a record of 53-23-1.

George "Reggie" Rawlings played with the Martinsburg team and is considered by many to be the best Blue Ridge League player ever. Photo courtesy of Robert Savitt.

The Blue Ridge League baseball schedule that ran in The Valley Spirit. Photo courtesy of Robert Savitt.

WWI

As the league proceeded forward, teams changed names. The Hagerstown team would have four names in 15 years– Blues, Terriers, Champs, and Hubs. Teams left the league because of financial pressures, and new teams in new towns took their places. The new towns that played in the Blue Ridge League were Waynesboro, Pa.; Cumberland, Md.; and Westernport, Md./Piedmont, W. Va., although the league never had more than six teams at one time.

Entering its 1918 season, the Blue Ridge League faced two major problems. The World War I draft continued to make soldiers and sailors of many of the players, making it hard to field a team. It was happening in other professional leagues as well, but the higher-level teams drew from the lower-class leagues to fill their holes, which left leagues like the Blue Ridge League struggling to find players

The Blue Ridge League was the only Class D league that

even attempted a season, and it had only four teams. To make matters worse, the Spanish Flu sickened and sometimes killed both players and fans.

Clyde Barnhart started professional baseball playing for Frederick's Blue Ridge League team, but he made the jump into the Major League and play for the Pittsburgh Pirates. Photo courtesy of Robert Savitt.

Because of these problems, the Blue Ridge League's 1918 season ended after only three weeks and did not resume play until 1920 once players returned from the war and got back into playing baseball.

Things seemed to improve after the war. The Blue Ridge League gained a reputation as a well-run league, although it continued to be difficult to make professional baseball financially viable in small cities.

The 1921 Frederick Hustlers won the Blue Ridge League pennant that year. Photo Courtesy of Robert Savitt.

The Farm System

Though the Major League teams recruited players from the Blue Ridge League, the teams remained independent. However, in the late-1920's, the teams began agreeing to Major League ownership. Not only did the Major League team financially support the small Blue Ridge League teams, but they lent the prestige of their names to the smaller teams.

"The Blue Ridge League was the pioneer in the formation of the farm system," Savitt said.

Of the six teams in the league, Hagerstown was the only

team that remained unaffiliated with a Major League team.

The Blue Ridge League also pioneered playing night games under bright lights and playing games on Sunday. The latter actually led to players being arrested for violating Blue Laws.

Dozens of players went on to play in the Major League. Three future Hall of Famers took their first steps in the Blue Ridge League: pitcher Lefty Grove (Martinsburg, 1920), outfielder Hack Wilson (Martinsburg, 1921-'22) and umpire Bill McGowan (1917). Bill Allington (Chambersburg, 1926), the most successful manager in the All-American Girls Professional Baseball League, was also inducted rest of the AAGPBL.

The Lone Mission of Coxey's Navy

Armies passed through Hancock during the Civil War, but never a navy. That changed on the afternoon of April 18, 1894, when Coxey's Navy arrived and occupied the town for a night.

Coxey's Navy was a group of unemployed workers that formed in Massillon, Ohio, under the direction of Jacob Coxey. The official name of the group was the Commonweal of Christ, but most people referred to it as Coxey's Army. That was until the group boarded a pair of canal boats in Cumberland the day before, and the Army became the Navy.

Jacob Coxey commanded the first boat which was renamed *Good Roads*. It got underway around 12:30 p.m. on Apr. 17. "Sandy" Leitch supplied travel music on the bagpipes. The second boat, renamed *J. S. Coxey*, got started about twenty minutes later under the command of Carl Browne. The men of Coxey's Army had voted for Browne to lead them a few days earlier. On this boat, the Commonweal band played the travel music.

The reporters covering the event were forced to rent their own boat and follow the navy down the canal.

The group planned to march to Washington D.C. where Coxey would present his petition to Congress of his ideas for a national program of building and repairing roads that would also solve the national unemployment problem. The group had started its march with much fanfare, leaving Massillon on Easter Sunday, Mar. 25, and had made their way slowly eastward. Traveling by boat from Cumberland allowed to group to make up lost time from the slow walk. The group covered three days of marching in 28 hours on the canal.

Jacob Coxey

Stories of disorderly conduct plagued the men as they traveled, making many communities leery upon seeing them approach. This included the officials of Washington, D.C. The city commissioners planed for how to deal with the growing army. "If Coxey's army was met at the edge of the District by the police or militia and forbidden to enter the men probably would skirt around in small detachments and enter the city by night, inaugurating a reign of terror among women and children, unless the militia were kept patrolling the border," the *Cumberland Evening Times* reported.

While the men in the army did not act so badly, the army did face deprivation and slow passage on the very roads they hoped to repair.

Infighting over leadership of the group had led to factions forming and even a mutiny as the two leaders vied for control of the army. Browne, whom Coxey had appointed to lead the group, was ousted from leadership and a group led by Unknown Smith took control. No one knew the man's name, and he refused to give it to reporters, so they called him "Unknown Smith."

Though the group was named after Coxey, he rarely traveled with it. Instead, he traveled ahead and slept in rooms while the men who followed him were generally forced to sleep outside.

Browne's ouster lasted for a day until Coxey caught up with the army in Cumberland. Once he did, Coxey had Browne reinstated, and the army voted to expel Smith and his small group of supporters.

This came back to haunt Coxey in Hancock when he found out Unknown Smith had been in town the previous night, saying he and his companion were advance agents for the army. They addressed a crowd, took up a collection, and left on the morning of the Apr. 18. "Private charity that might have gone to them had been drained before the army's arrival by two traitors in the camp," the *Cumberland Evening Times* reported.

So Coxey's men ate cheese and crackers from their stores for dinner. However, some men must have had money because there were reports of men from the group doing plenty of drinking in town that evening.

Meanwhile, Coxey issued a complaint about Smith and his group, which allowed the Washington County Sheriff to take action.

Coxey's Army sets out from Cumberland, traveling along the C&O Canal on two canal boats. Photo courtesy of the National Park Service.

While in Hancock, an odd situation developed when the Fayette County, Pa., sheriff arrived and arrested a man in the navy named Mason for the murder of the chief engineer in a Connellsville, Pa., coke plant. During a strike at the plant, a mob beat the engineer and threw him from the top of a tipple. Witnesses identified Mason as the man who threw the engineer to his death, but it turned out that another man named Mason had been arrested for the same thing in Franklin County, Pa. Both men were taken into custody until authorities could sort out the situation.

The navy stayed in Hancock three hours before resuming their journey down the Chesapeake and Ohio Canal. They left the town with twenty-five more men than they arrived with. However, some of them were so drunk they had to walk on the towpath until they were sober for fear they would fall off the boats.

The canal boats arrived at the Cushwa Basin in Williamsport at 8 a.m. the following morning, and Coxey's Navy once again became Coxey's Army.

"The men swarmed over the sides of the boats to the towpath and to a green pasture field near by. As soon as they got the kinks out of their legs and had a bit of the cold water of the canal dashed in their faces, they took the wagons, stock and provisions from the boats and made ready for breakfast," the *Baltimore Sun* reported. At this point, about 225 men made up Coxey's Army, although other groups were coming from different locations to converge on Washington as well.

Before he had a chance to get his land legs, Coxey fell into the canal. "Undaunted, he laughed about getting wet and said he had plenty of dry clothes in his trunk. A reporter happened to be near him when he opened the one with his personal belongings, only to find that it was filled with dirty clothes. Naturally, Coxey was angry until he found out that Jesse was the culprit. Girls had found the young man attractive, and he had been borrowing his father's clothes to put on his best appearance." John Grant wrote in in his monograph, *Coxey's 38-Day March Through the Alleghenies in Search of Economic Justice.*

The men unloaded the canal boats and reassembled the wagons.

As the men rolled out of Williamsport, Coxey's Army ran into trouble from toll taker Jacob McKusker, who sought to collect the toll for hundreds of men, wagons, and horses. McKusker told Coxey, "If Uncle Sam's entire army and navy wanted to pass his toll gate, they would have to pay the toll."

The group relented and paid the toll. The army continued on to Hagerstown, where they camped on Logan Hill. According to the *Baltimore Sun*, the army arrived in the city around 12:30 p.m. with banners flying and music playing. The group was not only made up of men on foot, but mounted on horses, driving wagons, and riding bicycles. The Hagerstown Police led them to their campsite. A canvas wall was erected around Camp Nazareth, and visitors were charged 10 cents a person to enter.

Coxey's Army on the road. Photo courtesy of the Library of Congress.

Hagerstown Mayor Keedy held a banquet at the Hamilton Hotel with Coxey as the guest of honor. The following morning, Coxey held a Sunday service at Camp Nazareth.

The army headed for Boonsboro the following day on Apr. 23 and sent a man ahead to pay the toll on the road.

"They passed through a thickly settled country and all along the march the roadway was lined with spectators. Marshal Browne rode at the head of the line with Jesse Coxey, and behind him came Mr. Coxey in his chaise," the *Baltimore Sun* reported.

They camped on South Mountain and crossed it the next morning. Frederick County Sheriff Zimmerman and thirty mounted deputies met the group at the county line and escorted them into Frederick.

From there, the group was able to meet its deadline date to get to Washington, where thousands of people lined the streets to watch them march through the city. However, things still did not go smoothly.

"Before the marchers could present their petition, the police rushed them, and Coxey and the other leaders were arrested for trampling on the grass," Harold Scott wrote in his book *Incredible, Strange, Unusual...*

Though the group failed that day, what they sought to achieve resonated with the public. Fifty years later, Coxey was finally able to read his speech from the Capitol steps. Grant also notes that many of Coxey's ideas became part of President Franklin Delano Roosevelt's New Deal Programs.

The Woodpecker vs. Fort Ritchie

Sitting atop South Mountain, Fort Ritchie helped save the world from the Nazis during World War II. However, the camp didn't fare as well against woodpeckers.

Fort Ritchie's history dates back to 1889 when the Buena Vista Ice Company of Philadelphia purchased 400 acres on South Mountain. The company developed the land and built lakes where it planned to cut ice from to ship to the surrounding cities for use as the refrigeration source in ice boxes. The first lake was built in 1901 and named Lake Royer. Buena Vista shipped out the ice on the Western Maryland Railroad, which ran through the area.

Business continued until the demand for ice dropped off due to the development of electric refrigeration, and the Buena Vista Ice Company eventually closed.

In 1926, the Maryland National Guard was looking for a location for a summer training camp. It chose the Buena Vista Ice Company property. Not only was the location isolated enough for the National Guard's training needs, it was located along the railroad, so it could be easily accessed and communications could be maintained using the telegraph line that already ran through the area.

The Maryland National Guard used the site from 1926 to 1942. On June 19, 1942, the U.S. Army took over the site for its Military Intelligence Training Center. During World War

II, 19,600 intelligence troops trained at the camp.

Despite the vast knowledge and intelligence training of these soldiers, woodpeckers managed to sabotage the camp, even if the interference lasted a short time.

In 1948, newspapers in Maryland and Pennsylvania ran stories about how woodpeckers were frustrating Col. Leland T. Reckford, the fort commander, with their attacks on power line poles.

An old postcard view of Barrick Avenue at Fort Richie.

"One woodpecker was so diligent in his attack on a pole that the first hard gust of wind the other day sent it crashing to the ground," the Hagerstown *Morning Herald* reported on November 9, 1948.

The 2,200-volt power line came down with the pole, causing outages in the area, including the camp.

"There are plenty of trees in the surrounding mountains, if the woodpeckers simply must release their emotions by pecking, camp officials point out," according to the *Morning Herald*.

Woodpeckers peck for three reasons, according to Ornithology.com. It uncovers insects, insect eggs, and larvae, which the woodpeckers eat. They drill holes in dead or dying trees to create nests. The hammering also serves as a type of communication to mark territory.

"This is why you might see a flicker pounding on a metal power pole or your house siding–to make the loudest sound he can, not to look for food or drill a hole, but to make a statement," according to the website.

Given the damage to the power line pole, it seems likely the woodpeckers used it create a nesting area, but instead, compromised the strength of the pole.

The newspapers don't note how the camp solved its woodpecker problem, but it wasn't mentioned again, nor were there any articles talking about additional falling power line poles.

Fort Ritchie closed in 1998 under the 1995 Base Realignment and Closure Commission.

The World's Largest Organ Manufacturer

When churches and other organizations want an organ with a rich, penetrating sound, they install a pipe organ. When they want one built to last, they chose M. P. Moller Organs. It was the largest manufacturer of pipe organs in the world for decades.

"The pipes used in the construction of a pipe organ range in size from pencil-thin ones several inches long to mammoth ones 32 feet in length. The smallest pipes are pitched so high that they are barely audible to the human ear; the largest so low and with such volume that their sound can shake a building. All of the pipes of an individual organ are divided into four 'families' – the strings, the diapasons, the woodwinds and the reeds. Some of Moller's most expert craftsmen are the men who "voice" these pipes to give them the pitch required. There are no stock sizes of pipes, all organs being custom designed, so each pipe is fashioned individually, whether from wood or metal," the *Hagerstown Daily Mail* reported in 1957.

Peter Mathias Moller was born in Denmark in 1854, but after serving a three-year apprenticeship to learn the mechanical trades, he emigrated to the United States at the age of seventeen.

He worked for the Derrick-Felgemaker Company, which

was the country's largest organ maker at the time.

After learning the craft, he developed his own ideas on how organs should be built. In particular, he had ideas on building a better wind chest. He opened his company in Philadelphia in 1875, and he set about building an organ for the 1876 Centennial Exposition, considered to be the first World's Fair. However, his need to earn money to support himself while he built his organ delayed his work. He didn't have it ready for the exposition, but when it was complete, people who heard it played thought the sound was superior.

He installed his first organ in the Swedish Lutheran Church in Warren, Pa., and it played there for over sixty years until the church was destroyed by fire in the 1940s.

A Greencastle, Pa., businessman lured Moller to that town 1877 with promises of financial assistance. Moller moved and opened his factory there, but the assistance never materialized.

In 1880, a delegation from Hagerstown convinced Moller to relocate his factory in that city.

The original Hagerstown Moller Organ Factory was enlarged six times before fire destroyed it in 1895. A new factory was built in downtown Hagerstown and continued to expand and grow.

According to various sources, the early Moller organs used mechanical action in the pipe chests that linked the console to the pipes by mechanical means. Moller contracted with supply houses to build these early instruments.

Later organs used tubular-pneumatic action for a brief time until the company adopted its own version of electro-pneumatic action in 1919.

He also built organs of varying sizes to fit just about any budget. This allowed country churches to have a superior-sounding Moller Organ as well as cathedrals in the country's largest cities.

Besides churches, theaters purchased a lot of organs to provide the musical soundtrack for motion pictures. Many organ companies had theaters as some of their largest customers. This all changed with the introductions of "talkies" in 1928. Movies started coming with their own music, and organs were no longer needed.

The old Moller Organ Company building in 2014. Photo courtesy of Wikimedia Commons.

"Many of the smaller companies that had turned out the organs used in the majority of theatres folded immediately, but Moller's, as always dependent upon sale of fine instruments to churches, continued to boom," the *Daily Mail* reported.

The first major contract the company won was to install an organ in the Cadet Chapel of the United States Military Academy at West Point, New York. This was Möller Opus 1200, and it was dedicated in 1911. With 14,000 pipes, it remains the largest all-pipe organ in a religious structure.

Due to his success with this organ, the Moller Pipe Organ Company went on to rebuild and expand the Naval Academy

Chapel organ in 1940 and build the Air Force Academy Chapel organ in 1963.

Moller died on April 13, 1937, from complications from pneumonia he had contracted during the winter and failed to recover fully from. He was eighty-two years old.

"No citizen of Hagerstown has left a greater impress or contributed more to the industrial, religious and civic life of the community, and none was more widely known or held in higher regard in all parts of the country," the *Daily Mail* reported.

Besides owning the Moller Organ Company, Peter Moller had spread his business interests throughout Hagerstown. He had bought the Crawford Automobile Company when it went into bankruptcy. He was one of the founders of the Home Builders Building and Loan Association. He sat on the boards of the Potomac Edison Company and Hagerstown and Frederick Railroad. He served as president of Hagerstown Trust, and he owned the Hotel Princess Dagmar and Moller Apartment Building.

The Moller Organ Company must have also been a fine place to work. In 1949, the *Daily Mail* reported that two employees, Harry Harbaugh and Charles DeLauder, were both in their 80s, and they had been working with Moller's since the company's early days in Hagerstown.

During WWII, the company shifted some of its business operations to serving as a subcontractor to Fairchild Aircraft making wings for the PT-19 trainer. They also made equipment for the United States Navy Bureau of Aeronautics.

After the war, Moller Organ Company moved to becoming a high-end manufacturer of organs. It saw success because of its sound quality and quicker delivery.

"The size of the building, its acoustical conditions, the location of the organ, the space available, the frequency of use and the scope of musical programming all have an influence on the organ's design," the *Daily Mail* reported. "For this reason, the creation of a Moller pipe organ is a considerable task and a highly individual undertaking."

By WWII, the company was the largest organ manufacturer in the world with annual revenues of $2.5 million, three times the size of the number two manufacturer.

Moller Opus 515 built in 1904 for St. Paul's Lutheran Church in Annville, Pa. It is now in First Christian Church in Albany, Ore. Photo courtesy of Wikimedia Commons.

"One does not normally find an organ manufacturer in every community, and the fact that the M. P. Moller Company, has become the world's largest manufacturer in this select field points out that this local firm holds a truly unique position in area industrial development," the *Daily Mail* reported in 1962.

In 1949, it employed 600 workers, four times as many workers as the number two manufacturer. "Among the jobs represented in this one factory are pipe-makers, machinists, toolmakers, painters, cabinetmakers, carpenters, pipe voicers, organ builders, console makers, electricians, draftsmen and engineers in a number of fields," according to the *Daily Mail*.

Moller organs can be found in all fifty states and many countries including Japan, South Africa, Denmark, England, Canada, Mexico, and the Virgin Islands. Not surprisingly, the highest concentration of Moller organs could be found in Washington County. Up until that point, 102 Moller organs had been installed in the county. Some churches had had as many as three Moller organs over the year.

By the 1980s, the company started using solid-state electronics for console components and other innovations. Competitors had embraced these innovations years earlier and gained ground on Moller.

The company closed in 1992. It was having labor problems and was more than $2 million in debt.

The last Moller organ installed was in the Chapel by the Sea of Fort Myers Beach, Fla. Many other churches weren't so lucky as they lost downpayments they had made toward organs they never received. More than $1 million in claims from 30 churches was lodged against the company.

Former employees and other investors tried to revive the company, but they all failed.

Over its 117 year history, the company made more than 12,000 instruments, including instruments in National Shrine of the Immaculate Conception in DC, Lincoln Center in NY. The largest Moller Organ in a church is the Opus 11739 in Calvary Church in Charlotte, N.C. installed in 1990. The largest Moller organ in a theater is in the Atlanta Fox Theatre.

When Did People Start Watching TV in the County?

Although the first television broadcast was made in 1928, it would be another twenty years before watching TV caught on in Washington County.

The catch with watching television in its early days was that you needed to live in an area where you could pick up a broadcast.

The early stations used a VHF (very high frequency) band. There were originally eighteen channels, but by 1948, there were only twelve (channels 2-13). In high population areas where there were more channels in use, this could create interference. So the channels tended to be broadcast in those areas rather than the more rural area.

The government began experimenting with UHF (ultra high frequency) broadcasting in the late 1940s. Its success led to the expansion of stations into areas that rarely had television reception because of the transmission interference.

This is also when television gained popularity in Washington County.

"You could probably find a half-residents claiming that they owned the first television set in the Hagerstown area, if you judge by conflicting claims for pioneering in auto ownership or radio reception," the *Hagerstown Daily Mail* reported in 1973.

In trying to determine when television first came to the county, the newspaper looked at advertisements in the newspaper.

"A search of newspapers during the Christmas shopping season of 1948 failed to turn up any firms offering television sets as holiday merchandise. By December of 1949, several local stores were advertising television sets for sale, and one establishment was running a daily advertisement in the classified pages about its repair services," the newspaper reported.

The newspaper admitted that this didn't mean some people didn't own television in the county prior to 1948, but it would have been difficult to receive a station. It's no coincidence that television popularity in the county jumped when it became easier to watch a broadcast on a new UHF station.

One person interviewed by the newspaper believed the Elk Club might have had the first television set in downtown Hagerstown. "He remembers it as a type which threw the image like a movie projector instead of offering direct viewing on a built-in screen, and it required an adjustment at the rear of the chassis every time channels were changed," according to the *Daily Mail*.

Around this time, advertisements can also be seen in the newspaper for George Hamilton's Mountain Rest Tourist Court on Dual Highway outside of Hagerstown. It encouraged people to come eat dinner and watch sports broadcasts on its television in 1947.

The oldest reference to a television set in the county is vague. A 1940 ad in the *Morning Herald* for M. P. Moller Music Store on S. Potomac Street advertised the RCA Victrola Model U-40 with a "television attachment and built-in loop antenna." However, images of the model don't show a television screen, so this might mean something different from what it sounds like, or it may mean some people in the county could receive television broadcasts. In 1940, though, they would not have able to use this feature of the Victrola.

An ad for the RCA Victrola that had an antenna "Designed for use with Television Attachment."

S and T Television on West Washington Street advertised itself in 1949 as "Hagerstown's first exclusive television store."

Despite the growing popularity of television in the county, Washington County didn't get its own television station until December 1, 1969, when WHAG went on the air on channel 25.

"In a sense, Channel 25 will be Western Maryland's first television station. Cumberland has Channel 52 on the air but only in a limited capacity," the *Daily Mail* reported.

Until this time, residents got their television from Cumberland, Chambersburg, and other surrounding counties. The closest station was WCHA, channel 46, in Chambersburg, which went on the air in 1953.

Today, WHAG not broadcasts as WDVM.

Washington County Enters the Auto Age

While Crawford Automotive is often considered Washington County's only car manufacturing company because it built cars in the county for more than two decades, the Pope Automobile Group had already been operating a year when Crawford Automotive started.

Forms of the automobile had been around for more than a century in 1904, but people still considered them a novel form of transportation. Travel was not much faster than a man on a horse could trot and the ride was still as rough given the state of roads at that time.

Alexander Pope was a Civil War veteran who lived in Massachusetts. He invested his modest saving in shoemakers' supplies, which returned more than ten times what he invested. He then invested that money in bicycles. He started by importing bicycles from England, but then he began manufacturing his own designs when a bicycling craze hit America in the late 1800s.

With his success with bicycles, he diversified into automobiles in 1896 and founded the Pope Motor Carriage Company. He soon began expanding by opening small firms to manufacture specific models of automobiles.

Pope was one of the first auto manufacturers to use mass

production practices in his companies. In 1900, Pope's automobile factories produced more motor vehicles than any other factory in the world.

An advertisement for Pope Manufacturing that featured the Pope Tribune.

He opened the Pope-Tribune plant (Pope had also built a bicycle called the Tribune in Massachusetts) in Hagerstown in 1903. It was set up in the old Crawford bicycle factory, which may have inspired George Crawford to start his own car company the following year. The building was located on the Baltimore and Ohio Railroad with its own sidings that made it easy to ship newly manufactured vehicles all over the country. The company soon added a water tower and another story to the building.

Alexander placed his son, Harold, in charge of the manufacturing operation. The plant built the Pope-Tribune, a single-cylinder runabout. The car cost between $500 and $650 (roughly $22,300 to $29,000 today) for the base model with a six-horsepower engine (some racing go-karts use a six-horsepower engine). It was the least expensive of the Pope automobiles. Other models included the Toledo, the Hartford, the Robinson, and the Waverley.

The *Hagerstown Morning Herald* noted on January 27, 1904, that Julia H. Hamilton was one of the first people to purchase a Pope Tribune.

The *Morning Herald* reported every Tribune that rolled out of the factory had been quality tested. "Every Tribune is given a thorough test, including the running of the engine a distance equivalent to about 200 miles, before it is shipped from the factory. As the grounds at the Pope plant are not large enough for this testing the Pope people have been using turnpikes leading out of Hagerstown quite extensively."

However, the company was close to shutting down by June when a slew of new state laws regarding automobiles went into effect. One law kept the cars from being tested on turnpikes. Things eventually settled down and production picked up. At its peak, the plant employed 300 people.

The plant also manufactured bicycles. A 1906 article in

the *Morning Herald* noted Pope Manufacturing made improvements at the plant so it could build 25,000 bicycles and 350 automobiles that year.

As cars continued to grow in size and speed, people lost interest in the Tribune despite its affordability. The company also tried marketing larger and more-expensive versions of the car. The last models the company produced had four-cylinder 16- or 20-hp engines. They sold for $1,750 (roughly $70,000). A 30-hp model sold for $2,750 (roughly $110,300 today).

A 1904 Pope-Tribune taking part in the 2009 London Brighton veteran car run. Photo courtesy of Wikimedia Commons.

The company continued building cars until November 1908 when the plant closed. The Montross Metal Casket Company took over the facility. Many of the 125 men at the plant transferred to a Pope plant in Westfield, Mass. This is also where the equipment was shipped. The plant there manufactured bicycles.

One problem appeared to have been too much clerical staff. An article in the *Mail* reported, "A former employe stated that the clerical force was a great if not greater than the working force, and that when a piece of material was needed for a job it required more time to get it coming through the varied channels than it took to complete the job."

The Pope Manufacturing Company filed for bankruptcy in 1915. Although the company reorganized the following year, it no longer made automobiles.

Although rare, the Pope Tribune is a piece of Washington County's heritage.

Building a Better Road

As road transportation improved in the United States, the number of wagons using roads and their weight increased. Road durability became important. No one wanted to have to free wagons from muddy bogs that dirt roads could turn into during a storm or try and travel for miles over rutted roads. Travel over cobblestones was barely any better.

Around 1820, John Loudon McAdam, a Scottish engineer, developed a new road construction technique that was better and cheaper than conventional methods of the time. It came to be called macadam after the man who invented it, and Washington County was the first place in North America to have this type of modern road.

McAdam started thinking about how roads could be improved in 1787 when he became a trustee of the Ayrshire Turnpike in Scotland. He moved to Bristol, England, in 1802 and became the commissioner for paving in 1806. A decade later, he was elected surveyor-general of roads for the turnpike trust.

Not only was he responsible for 149 miles of road, he could put his new construction method to the test. It was actually simpler than other methods of the time that required layers of large rock as a foundation. It was also more effective at protecting the roadway.

McAdam used smaller rocks with only a slight rise from the edges of the road to the center. The size of the rocks needed to be smaller than the width of a wheel, which was typically four-inches wide. The smaller angular rocks acted like a solid mass and created a smoother surface.

A painting showing the construction of the first American macadam near Boonsboro. Courtesy of Wikimedia Commons.

Only a few years after McAdam introduced it, macadam was introduced in North America on the Boonsborough Turnpike Road between Hagerstown and Boonsboro. This was the last unimproved section of road that extended the National Road east from Cumberland to Baltimore.

"Stagecoaches using the road in winter needed 5 to 7 hours of travel to cover 10 miles," according to Curbstone.com.

The builders decided to employ the new macadam process. "Construction specifications for the turnpike road incorporated those set forth by John Loudon McAdam of Scotland," Curbstone.com reports. "After side ditches were dug, large rocks were picked and raked, then were broken 'so as not to exceed 6 ounces in weight or to pass a two-inch ring.' Compacting work for each of the three layers was quickened using a cast-iron roller, instead of allowing for compacting under traffic."

This last item differed somewhat from McAdam's process that used the wagons traveling the road to compact it over time.

The success of the road led to macadam being used to repave the National Pike. The 73 miles of road were repaved from 1825 to 1830.

Later engineers took improved on the idea using things like water and tar to keep up with road needs as transportation continued improving. Even today's more-popular asphalt uses some of the principles of macadam, such as compacting small aggregates on a slight incline. The big difference is that asphalt mixes the aggregates in tar before laying it while tar-sealed macadam sprayed tar on the finished road surface.

Acknowledgements

I wanted to thank all of those people who helped me put together the *Secrets of Washington* together. The longer I work as a writer, the more I realize that while one person may publish a book, the effort is much richer when others assist.

COVID-19 created a huge difficulty as I wrote this book. Each of the Secrets books is made up of previously published stories and original stories. This book required more original stories than usual at a time when libraries, museums, and historical societies were closed. I found myself digging deeper looking for sources and verification for stories.

One great local resource in this regard is the Western Maryland Historical Library (whilbr.org). It has tons of information and pictures about historical topics in Washington, Allegany, and Garrett counties.

I'd also like to thank Deb Spalding, publisher of *The Catoctin Banner*; Guy Fletcher, editor of *Frederick Magazine;* Holly Smith, former editor of *Maryland Life*; and Angela Niessner, editor of Hagerstown Magazine. All of them have been willing to publish my history articles over the years.

Finally, I'd like to thank Grace Eyler for not only another great-looking cover but also being able to create the template for the Secrets series.

I have probably missed someone who I'll remember after this book goes to print. If so, it's not because I didn't appreciate your input. I sometimes get confused juggling all of the projects that I do. If I did leave you out, mention it to me.

Hopefully, by the time this book is published, the worst of COVID will be behind us. Take care of yourself.

James Rada, Jr.
January 1, 2021

About the Author

James Rada, Jr. is an Amazon.com bestselling author of historical fiction and non-fiction history. They include the popular books *Strike the Fuse, Canawlers,* and *Battlefield Angels: The Daughters of Charity Work as Civil War Nurses.*

He lives in Gettysburg, Pa., where he works as a freelance writer. James has received numerous awards from the Maryland-Delaware-DC Press Association, Associated Press, Maryland State Teachers Association, Society of Professional Journalists, and Community Newspapers Holdings, Inc. for his newspaper writing.

If you would like to be kept up to date on new books being published by James or ask him questions, he can be reached by e-mail at *jimrada@yahoo.com.*

To see James' other books or to order copies on-line, go to *www.jamesrada.com.*

PLEASE LEAVE A REVIEW

If you enjoyed this book, please help other readers find it. Reviews help the author get more exposure for his books. Please take a few minutes to review this book at *Amazon.com* or *Goodreads.com.* Thank you, and if you sign up for my mailing list at *jamesrada.com*, you can get FREE ebooks.

WANT TO KNOW MORE SECRETS?

Find out the little-known stories and hidden history of Maryland and Pennsylvania with the Secrets series from James Rada, Jr.

Available wherever books are sold.

CRITICAL ACCLAIM FOR THE WORKS OF JAMES RADA, JR.

The Last to Fall

"Authors Jim Rada and Richard Fulton have done an outstanding job of researching and chronicling this little-known story of those Marines in 1922, marking it as a significant moment in Marine Corps history."

- *GySgt. Thomas Williams*
Executive Director
U.S. Marine Corps Historical Company

"Original, unique, profusely illustrated throughout, exceptionally well researched, informed, informative, and a bit iconoclastic, "The Last to Fall: The 1922 March, Battles, & Deaths of U.S. Marines at Gettysburg" will prove to be of enormous interest to military buffs and historians."

- *Small Press Bookwatch*

Saving Shallmar

"But Saving Shallmar's Christmas story is a tale of compassion and charity, and the will to help fellow human beings not only survive, but also be ready to spring into action when a new opportunity presents itself. Bittersweet yet heartwarming, Saving Shallmar is a wonderful Christmas season story for readers of all ages and backgrounds, highly recommended."

- *Small Press Bookwatch*

Battlefield Angels

"Rada describes women religious who selflessly performed life-saving work in often miserable conditions and thereby gained the admiration and respect of countless contemporaries.

In so doing, Rada offers an appealing narrative and an entry point into the wealth of sources kept by the sisters."
- *Catholic News Service*

Between Rail and River

"The book is an enjoyable, clean family read, with characters young and old for a broad-based appeal to both teens and adults. Between Rail and River also provides a unique, regional appeal, as it teaches about a particular group of people, ordinary working 'canawlers' in a story that goes beyond the usual coverage of life during the Civil War."
- *Historical Fiction Review*

Canawlers

"A powerful, thoughtful and fascinating historical novel, Canawlers documents author James Rada, Jr. as a writer of considerable and deftly expressed storytelling talent."
- *Midwest Book Review*

"James Rada, of Cumberland, has written a historical novel for high-schoolers and adults, which relates the adventures, hardships and ultimate tragedy of a family of boaters on the C&O Canal. ... The tale moves quickly and should hold the attention of readers looking for an imaginative adventure set on the canal at a critical time in history."
- *Along the Towpath*

October Mourning

"This is a very good, and very easy to read, novel about a famous, yet unknown, bit of 20th Century American history. While reading this book, in your mind, replace all mentions of 'Spanish Flu' with 'bird flu.' Hmmm."
- *Reviewer's Bookwatch*

www.ingramcontent.com/pod-product-compliance
Lightning Source LLC
Chambersburg PA
CBHW071040080526
44587CB00015B/2700